Sir William Johnson

The Man and his Influence

Sir William Johnson
The Man and his Influence

David S. Igneri, Ph.D.

RIVERCROSS PUBLISHING, INC.
NEW YORK

Copyright © 1994 by David S. Igneri

ISBN: 0-944957-49-8

Library of Congress Catalog Card Number: 94-31216

First Printing

Library of Congress Cataloging-in-Publication Data

Igneri, David S., 1944-
  Sir William Johnson : the man and his influence / David S. Igneri.
    p.   cm.
  Includes bibliographical references.
  ISBN 0-944957-49-8 : $15.95
  1. Johnson, William, Sir, 1715-1774.   2. Indians of North
America—Government relations—To 1789.   3. United
States—History—French and Indian War, 1755-1763.   4. Colonial
administrators—United States—Biography.   5. Colonial administra-
tors—Great Britian—Biography.   I. Title.
E195.J63I38   1994
973.2'6—dc20
                                                    94-31216
                                                       CIP

TABLE OF CONTENTS

INTRODUCTION

Throughout the span of Colonial American history, many leaders rose to important positions and helped the British dominate the North American continent. That their eventual victory was only to last a generation in no way lessens their efforts or their service to their country. Colonial officials fought battles for Britain or for the British Crown, and indirectly laid the foundation for a new nation. They were generally loyal British citizens, yet they were also, in many ways, Americans.

One of the most important characters in colonial history was William Johnson. Born in Ireland in 1715, he emigrated to America at the age of twenty-two. He settled in the Mohawk Valley of New York, approximately twenty-five miles from the present city of Schenectady. Johnson soon began to trade with the Indians of the area, especially the Six Nations of the Iroquois Confederation. In 1746, Governor George Clinton appointed him Colonel of the Six Nations and five years later, made him a member of the governor's council.

The English had already fought three colonial wars against the French for control of the North American continent when, in 1754, the final conflict began. This conflict, known as the French and Indian War in the colonies and the Seven Years War in Europe, was an international confrontation. France would ultimately lose all of its North American territory and Britain would, almost overnight, become undisputed master of this former empire. Possibly one of the factors which contributed to the British victory was that the Six Nations of the powerful Iroquois Confederation largely remained neutral, or fought with them against their French foes.

One possible explanation for the Iroquois loyalty, especially the Mohawks, did not side with the French, as my volume will reveal, was the influence of Sir William Johnson. Sir William had traded with them for years, cohabited with at least two Mohawk maidens, and attained fast friendships with many famous Mohawk leaders. The Mohawks and the other nations of the Confederation respected and trusted Sir William implicitly. He was perceived as their great and loyal friend who was also the ultimate frontiersmen. Possibly, he understood their problems better than any other whiteman.

In 1755, Johnson was appointed sole superintendent of the Indian region north of the Carolinas and the Ohio River, and later that year, was commissioned a major general in the British army. He wanted the support of his Native American friends. He ultimately acquired this by the use of several methods at his disposal. This influence and eventual persuasion by the famed New Yorker, influenced the outcome of the French and Indian War.

The hypothesis in this study is that Sir William Johnson's influence with the Iroquois, especially the Mohawks, but also on other Indians, influenced the outcome of the war. A case will be built to substantiate this theoretical framework by thoroughly researching the primary sources and using the secondary works to support this evidence. Historians have alluded to this hypothesis, but have not published evidence for it. Sir William Johnson, by his service as a diplomat and persuader, possibly changed the history of the western hemisphere because of the outcome of the French and Indian War. Also, my theory is simply that Johnson, by learning the Native American languages, customs and culture, dealt with the Indians better than anyone else. Indians either directly or indirectly made the British victorious and should be given credit for their help. Possibly this study will add a new dimension to the William Johnson story and reveal the true value of Native American support at the time.

The area discussed in this volume is confined to the northeastern part of North America. This is the section in which most of the battles occurred in the French and Indian War. Other areas, such as the Caribbean region are not mentioned.

This study is written in the form of a biography. It discusses William Johnson's early life and his life in colonial New York. It disagrees with some of the biographers of the great colonial leader and agrees with others. The study surveys the background of the Iroquois and of Johnson's respect for Native American culture. It traces his early military experience before the French and Indian War began. Finally it delves into the main part of my study by dealing with my hypothesis. The final conclusions will hopefully lead to further research on the subject.

Sir William Johnson

The Man and his Influence

CHAPTER 1

Early Life

The early eighteenth century was a period of turmoil between the European powers of Great Britain and France. King William's War had ended the former century, lasting from 1689-1697. Queen Anne's War followed after a few years, and ended in 1713.

Two years after this second colonial war, William Johnson was born of Irish parents at Smithtown, in Meath County, Ireland.[1] His early years were spent enjoying comfortable beginnings across the ocean from his future home in America. No one could have predicted his later influence on colonial American history.

> The lineage of William Johnson goes back to William McShane (anglicised to William Johnson) who married Anna, the daughter of James Fitz Simmons of Tullinally, Westmeath. They had a son, Christopher Johnson, who removed to Smithtown, County Meath, and was married to Anne, daughter of Michael Warren of Warrentown, County Meath, and sister of Vice Admiral Sir Peter Warren. To Christopher (died in 1763) and Anne Johnson (died in 1744) were born William, Peter Warren Johnson of Damartown, County Meath, John of Warrenstown, County Meath, and five daughters.[2]

Some writers have suggested that William Johnson was of very humble beginnings. In actuality, the Johnson family were of the gentry class of Ireland. These people were not of the highest class, but they held land on which tenants labored for a pittance[3]. The homes of the gentry class were probably comfortable, but were not luxurious. They could not compare with the best homes in the other parts of the British Isles[4]. Although the gentry were not rich, they were not wanting for basic needs.

The gentry of Ireland did suffer criticism during their time. They generally had tenants who lived on their property who led hard lives. These tenants lived in huts, rather than houses, built of dirt, straw and sticks wrought together[5]. These were ... "generally removed once a year, and consequently were migratory, and not so durable, as the carts and wagons of the wandering Tartars."[6] Also according to Samuel Madden, numbers of them had no

> chimney, either for want of wood or skill to build one, but vent the smoak like those of the Hottentots; and if we had a market, as Mr. Beauplon says, the Cossacks have for wooden chimnies ready made, our poor people have not a penny to buy one. As miserable as they look on the outside, the family within are full as wretched, half starved and half clad, so that there is an absolute necessity to lodge them better and use them to warmer cottages and cloathing and a cleanlier way of feeding and living, if we would have them cultivate their lands or manufacture to any purpose.[7]

Many times, the gentry did not always concern themselves with the conditions under which their tenants lived. This was the class into which William Johnson was born into in 1715. It was an Ireland that generally took advantage of the workers of the soil. Samuel Madden stated in 1738, that Irish landlords thought more of their horses than those who labored on their lands[8] If they had shown concern, Madden said, we should soon have droves of men, and labouring men instead of bullocks and sheep and find the wide difference in the profit by making use of them.[9]

William Johnson was, therefore, born to a comfortable Irish family. There is the possibility that he was descended from royalty on his father's side.[10] In any case, he definitely was fairly well to do considering that the majority of the people of Ireland at the time were bound to the soil. Young William may have helped with the care of his father's land. His father had an "estate of two hundred acres leased from the Earl of Fingall in 1728."[11]

At this time large estates in Ireland, had many farm animals and grew a number of crops. Potatoes were a main crop.[12] They were "planted to such a large extent ... " that all the dung in the country was applied to them."[13] Other crops included wheat, barley, oats, corn, and turnips.[14] Dairy cows and sheep were also numerous on these large estates.[15]

The estate of Christopher Johnson was slightly larger than other Irish farms of the period. Farms were commonly 100 to 300 acres with some as small as five acres, and some as large as 600.[16] The average in the whole country was probably about 160 acres.[17] William Johnson was one of eight children. He was probably the eldest because the genealogy mentions him first. This fact cannot be determined for certain, but was probably the case. Peter Warren Johnson, born in 1732, was a much younger brother, and John Johnson was very close to William's age.[18] Peter Warren's age is not mentioned in any of the documents.

Irish gentry families were generally close families who did the best they could to put their offspring on the path of the straight and narrow. The Johnson family undoubtedly wanted all their children to succeed in life. All the Johnson girls were married and led what was considered productive lives. The five sisters of William Johnson included Anne Johnson Dease, Bridget Johnson Sterling, Francis Johnson Plunkett, Ellis Johnson Fitzsimmons[19] and Catherine Johnson Farrell.[20]

3

Not a great deal is known of William Johnson's early life in Ireland. Smithtown, his birthplace, was a small hamlet not shown on many maps.[21] It was approximately thirty-six miles northwest of Dublin.[22] The land was not the best farm land. Much of the area of Meath was bog and wasteland.[23]

William Johnson grew up and experienced life as a youth in and near the land his family farmed. This land had, centuries before, been inhabited by Irish Kings of Meath.[24] When he was growing up, William probably climbed the same hills that ancient kings once roamed. He grew strong and big for his time, possibly close to six feet tall and had dark hair. [25] His photograph reveals a rather handsome and masculine individual who was probably very attractive to the young ladies of the neighborhood.

William was undoubtedly expected to achieve some form of distinction with his life and could have taken up any of the traditional occupations at hand. Boys could have chosen careers with the army, the navy, the church, or the land.[26] Why he did not choose any of these is a matter of conjecture. Instead, in 1737, he decided to go to America to manage his uncle Peter Warren's land.

A possible reason he left was to get ahead and get away from the drudgery of the farm life he had known as a boy. The thrill of adventure was probably motivation enough for a young man of twenty-two to seek out on his own.[27] However, it would appear that many letters from his uncle while in Ireland must have helped convince him.[28] Years later, this was revealed when, in 1753, William wrote to Oliver DeLancey. The letter stated in part:

> As to what dealings (if I may properly call them so) was between my Dr. Uncle and me, I never kept any acctt of. takeing it for grant, by the many letters he wrote me when yet in Ireland, by what he told me when he sent me from Boston to Settle certain Tract of Land in Warrensborough, and Supply me with all things necessary to carry on my Work.[29]

4

seems that this may have been enough motivation for young William to leave his home in Ireland and migrate to a new continent, a wild country where adventure and even wealth were possible. The documents say no more of why he left his homeland. However, legend has made up other reasons for his departure.[30] They are revealed here as possibilities, and because they may be of interest to readers and further researchers.

William Johnson, according to the early biographers, left Ireland because of a discouraging love affair. He even promised to send for his lover after he got to America.[31] The name of the young woman is not known, but the story goes ... "that, on account of an unfortunate love affaire, he was induced by his uncle to emigrate to America."[32] The previous account told by W. Max Reid may or may not be true, but was repeated and, although questioned by later writers, had further explanation. It states "that young Johnson, a noble figure of young manhood on the eve of departing for America, loved a sweet Colleen who was to have been his bride."[33] The marriage never took place because his parents were strongly set against it.[34]

As already stated, of William Johnson's motives for leaving his homeland are conjectural at best. The legend of his supposed love affair has no supporting evidence in later documents. All that can be said of the tale is that it makes a good story.

The records, documents, and letters, do not say much about what kind of person young William was when he was in Ireland. It can be guessed from his later life that he must have been very sexually oriented. His relationships as a mature man in New York suggests that he may have been against total commitment to one woman as a youth.[35] His later life would support the thesis that ... "the tale of the lost Irish sweetheart torn from him by parental harshness"[36] could not have been true.

The details of his life that preceded the supposed love affair are based on much more evidence. William Johnson had been somewhat of an unruly youth in his late teens, and cause his parents some concern. This may have influenced his coming to America years later, and could have been one reason why young William was put in the care of a family member such as his uncle Peter Warren.

At the age of fourteen, the Johnson family sent young William to the Academy of Newry to study law and become a barrister. "In his seventeenth year, or about the middle of his third year at the Academy, his curriculum ended suddenly in a peremptory expulsion."[37] The explanation for this socially disgraceful event has been attributed to the attempt on the part of the Moderator or teacher to chastise him ... "which resulted in failure, disastrous to the pedagogue and dismissal to young William."[38] The strong minded youth was also "taken before a magistrate on a charge of aggravated assult and battery fined seven guineas, and 'put on the limits' for twenty one days."[39]

When William returned home after his punishment, his aging father, then about sixty, gave him the beating that the moderator had failed to administer[40] The flagellation which William suffered or endured must not have hurt the young man very much.[41] He undoubtedly was far physically superior to his old and crippled parent, ...[42] but showed respect in taking the punishment like a man.

The years between William's seventeenth birthday until he was in his early twenties were uneventful. He read law and history and worked as a magistrate in his father's office. He was even listed to take an examination in 1737 for admission as a junior barrister.[43] He never took this examination because of his offer to come to America.

It would appear that young William was put in the charge of his uncle Peter to help him find success in life. William may have become successful without outside help if he had remained in Ireland in the law profession. However, his strong will, his love for the ladies, and his physical prowess made him beyond the control of his elderly and crippled father.

Peter Warren was born in 1703 and, thus was only twelve

years older than William. He was the son of Michael Warren, a Catholic, but was raised by Rear Admiral Lord Aylmer as a protestant, after his father's early death.[44] Peter joined the navy at an early age, and became a captain at the age of twenty-four.

Peter Warren became the most distinguished member of his clan. He rose to the rank of Admiral[45] and gained wealth by marrying into the DeLancy-VanCortlant family of New York. Peter and Susannah DeLancy were married in 1731. He soon owned land in New York City, now Greenwich Village, and took part in land speculation in other areas.

In 1736, Captain Warren purchased 13,000 acres on the Mohawk River from Mrs. Cosby [46]. Mrs. Cosby was the widow of the former governor of New York, William Cosby. No doubt, Peter's family connections put him in touch with the lady, who made a quick sale.

> Captain Warren had made a very Great purchase of Mrs. Cosby at Boston 13000a of the Govrs Land at Trokenonder Hill for 110£ . How she became so Infatuated I know not, Sure it could be so Trifling a Sum ready money That Bewitched her but so it is which being done I Suppose The Captn will have no thoughts at present abot getting any other Tract, and I understand as much from The Chief Justice the other day talking upon This Subject.[47]

Very shortly after purchasing the aforementioned land, Captain Peter Warren offered his nephew a chance to manage it. Young William thus decided to leave Ireland at the tender age of twenty-two to take up a new life on the American frontier. He came to Boston in 1737 ...[48] and he brought with him twelve families who were recruited purposely to live on his uncle's land.[49] The group who came and met Captain Warren included William's sister Catherine and his cousin, Michael Tyrrell.[50]

Many of the early biographers assumed that from Boston, William's party went to New York and then up the Hudson

River to their destination. These accounts even have young William spending the winter in New York. As Max Reid stated:

> Late in the summer of 1737 he sailed for America arriving in New York as guest of his aunt Sir Peter Warren's wife.
>
> Lady Warren was the daughter of Stephen DeLancy, one of the richest merchants in New York, whose family held leadership in the most refined and aristocratic society of the provincial metropolis. It was in this social environment William passed the winter, and it is said that he bore himself with tact, dignity and grace worthy of wider experience and maturer years.[51]

Augustus Buell also wrote of William Johnson spending time in New York City and then going up the Hudson River in the spring of 1738.[52] He stated:

> As soon as navigation was opened in the North River in the spring of 1738, Johnson proceeded to Albany with a sloop-load of implements for subduing the forest, a set of mill irons and a run of stone. He also took with him half a dozen mechanics of various trades.[53]

In their biographies, modern historians Milton Hamilton[54] and Thomas Flexner[55] do not mention that William Johnson spent time in New York after landing in Boston. Hamilton reasons that supplies were bought in Boston and would have been bought in New York if the party planned to stop there. The documents available today do not reveal that Johnson stayed in New York.[56] However, Augustus Buell did state that such evidence did exist at least at one time.[57]

The Johnson party probably went overland and by water from Boston to Albany.[58] Approaching Albany from the east, he would have seen the great homes of the patroons and then went into the town. We can imagine what Willliam saw from an account by Peter Kalm in 1770:

8

The houses of the town are very neat, and partly built of stones covered with shingles of white pine. Some are slated with tile from Holland, because the clay of this neighborhood is not considered fit for tiles. Most of the houses are built the old Frankish way, with the gable-end towards the street, except a few, which were recently built in the modern style. A great number of houses are built like those of New Brunswick, which I have described, the gable-end towards the street being of bricks and all the other walls of boards. The outside of the houses is never covered with lime or mortar, nor have I seen it practiced in any North American towns which I have visited; and the walls do not seem to be damaged by the weather. The eaves on the roofs reach almost to the middle of the street. The front doors are generally in the middle of the houses, and on both sides are porches with seats, on which during fair weather the people spent almost the whole day, especially on those porches which are in the shade. The people seem to move with the sun and the shade always keeping in the latter.

The streets are broad and some of them paved. In some parts they are lined with trees. The long streets are parallel to the river and the others intersect them in right angles. The street which goes between the two churches is five times broader than the others and serves as a marketplace. The streets upon the whole are very dirty because the people leave their cattle in them during the summer nights. There are two marketplaces in town, to which the country people come twice a week. There are no city gates here for the most part just open holes through which people pass in and out of town.[59]

Most of the inhabitants of Albany in the 1730's and even

later were of Dutch extraction.[60] William Johnson must have noticed this and understood that he would have to deal with these people in the future. Albany was only some forty miles from his final destination. Young William had to realize that he would need to get supplies from the city after he made his settlement near present day Schenectady.

The Johnson party probably left Albany and traveled to their homesite during the spring. They went overland to Schenectady and down the Mohawk River by boat. Almost immediately, William "proceeded diligently to improve and develop his uncle's estate."[61] It was called Warrensburg, after his uncle. The land "was sold off in farms of 150 to 300 acres, and settlement was rapid."[62]

Young William began also to trade with the local inhabitants soon after arriving at Warrensburg. This had been encouraged by his uncle, Captain Peter Warren.[63] Warren mentioned his faith in his nephew by stating that "his diligence and application will put him in a good way."[64]

Captain Warren assisted William Johnson's efforts to make a success out of Warrensburg. He had his brother-in-law, James DeLancey, act as William's banker to help finance the venture and help speculate on land purchases for the Captain.[65] Thus, it seems quite obvious that within a short time after arriving at Warrensburg, William Johnson was managing his uncle's affairs very well and also making a name for himself. As William stated in a letter dated May 10th, 1739:

> People here are mad. Every day purchasing land,
> and Surveying so that land must be verry dear in a
> Short time; as to my keeping in well with all people
> you may Assure you Self of it, Dr. Uncle for I daresay
> I have the good will of all people wt. soever, and
> much respect, Verry much of yr. Acctt. and my Own
> Behavior, wh I trust in God I shall always
> Continue.[66]

William spent five years at Warrensburg from 1738 to 1743.[67] However, ... "he never intended to make it his permanent home, nor was he content with the occupation of agent for a landlord."[68] Shortly thereafter, William purchased several thousand acres of his own, north of the Mohawk River. Here, he would build his own house and begin his own life in colonial New York.

Uncle Peter Warren was not pleased with William's decision to purchase his own land. This can be discerned in a letter dated May 10th, 1739, which also describes William's intentions for the land.

> Dear Uncle
> I had < the favour of yours of the 20th of April > wherein I find you are displeased < att my purchasing the land, > Which in Everry Bodys Opinion< is a good Bargain, and Can any > time I please Sell it for the Money< and More So that I hope Dr. Uncle yl. not continue yr. Opinion> when yu. See it and know> My Design (wh. is this) to have a Carefull Honest < Man there > Who will Manage the farm, wh will at least< clear I am Sure > 30 Annum, Moreover the Chief thing is a < fine Creek to build > a Saw Mill on, haveing Loggs Enough att hand, < half of wh. Creek> belongs to Me, so that I intend after a little time, < please God, to > build a Mill there. So that the Income of that may Enable me < the beter> to go on in the World, tho I must Acknowledge Dr. Uncle that < wt. > great favours yu. Were pleased to do me, was a Sufficient Beginnings And am wth all the Gratitude Imaginable contented wth. it, and <for> the future shall be no way Expensive nore troublesome to you.[69]

William Johnson acquired title to the land in 1741. He soon built a stone house there, known as Mount Johnson. In 1755, it was surrounded by a palisade and renamed Fort Johnson.[70] This structure is still standing near the city of Amsterdam today.

William built a sawmill and a gristmill on his newly acquired property. It was no wonder that uncle Peter Warren was apprehensive and believed that "William intended to give up the charge of his estate and set up business for himself."[71] Johnson ultimately pacified his uncle by assuring him that, no matter what he did on his own, he would still look after the elder's business interests. He even assured his uncle, in 1739, that "As to my Moveing over where I made the purchase to live there I never had the least Notion in the World of it."[72] However, William also informed his uncle of the great prospects the purchase had for his future business. He stated

> It would be the properest place on the Whole River
> for a Store house and Shop in the Winter, by reason
> of all the High Germans passing by that way in the
> Winter, and all the upper Nations of Indians, whose
> trade is pritty Valluable, But I will talk no more abt.
> it until I have the pleasure of seeing yu.[73]

It is obvious that although he did not move from his uncle's land until 1743, that he had plans to do that at a much earlier time. In fact, by 1741, he was developing his own land and planning his own future. For the most part, the five years he spent at Warrensburg were uneventful. It is said that during that time he learned the skills that would make him a success later in life. Young William, for instance, learned the way of the frontier. He learned the rudiments of being a trapper, a trader, and a merchant. Much of his time was spent learning the ways of the Six Nations of Iroquois Indians. Very early on William realized his relationship with the Native Americans would influence his success in the future.

William Johnson went into business for himself after 1743 when he moved onto his own land. He still managed his uncle's interests and inherited Peter Warren's remaining land in 1752, after the older man's death.[74]

When he moved to his own land, William had many acres cleared for farming. He brought over approximately sixty Scotch-Irish families to work his land and had log homes waiting for them.[75] He began selling goods to anyone in his area who would buy. Much of the correspondence of the period has to do with the buying or selling of goods. An example is a letter of June 7th, 1745, approximately two years after he had moved to Mount Johnson. The letter to William Johnson from Edward Holland stated:

> Dear Sir:
> I Recd yours of ye < 20th past, with the Hogshd of Peltry > and boundle of Skins which < are Shipt on board of the > Antelope, who I dont believe will Sail < this Month, > Mr. Walters being Determin'd not < to let go till > he can have 2 or 3 opportunitys to write home for Insurance.[76]

This passage reveals that William Johnson, by the middle 1740's, was well set up as a merchant and trader who had many agents working to make him a man of affairs. Additional supportive evidence is contained in the letter. It states that Edward Holland wanted to be able to send William Johnson's crops to any market that would pay the best price. Holland stated

> nither would I have you confine me to any Particular Market, as they very frequently Vary You may rest asshured that I shall Consult your Interest in the same Manner as I would my own therefore would have you to Let me Judge for you in that Case where to send it to.[77]

There was only one missing ingredient in William Johnson's life as of the late 1730's. At Warrensburg, in the period when he was thinking of having his own place, William Johnson took his first wife. She supposedly came to him in 1739. Her name was Catherine Weissenberg. The birth dates of his children with her were 1739, 1740, and 1742.[78] All three were born before he left Warrensburg for Mount Johnson.

Catherine Weissenberg was an indentured servant who was a runaway from New York and probably joined friends in the Mohawk Valley.[79] She was supposedly a dark-haired German beauty to whom William was attracted, to, and thus took her

as a mate. There is no evidence that a formal marriage ceremony ever took place. Max Reid does state that William married her after she had his first child.[80] Also, a letter from
Daniel Claus to John Johnson of July 3, 1776 mentions the
marriage. It states

> 'Guy and I were at the Heralds Office in London And
> found your late father's Title entered in print in a
> book of heraldry but not his Arms for want as it
> says of knowing his descent his Marriage and law-
> full Issue. Now if you choose to have it completed it
> can be done for you by sending an attested Copy of
> his Marriage Certificate, the Issue by that Marriage
> and your Marriage and Issue with a Copy of the
> Arms.'[81]

William Johnson refers to Catherine as his wife in his will
and states he expects her to be buried alongside him. In the
same will, he refers to Mary Brant as his housekeeper and
separates his children into legitimate and natural.[82] Because
we believe that William Johnson was an honest man, we must,
therefore, feel that sometime during his relationship with
Catherine, he must have married her.[83]

Not much more is known about Catherine Weissenberg. It
was assumed by the early biographers that she died about
1750, but possibly lived until 1759, the year Mary Brant is first
mentioned in the Johnson papers.

In the middle 1740's, William Johnson lived at Mount
Johnson with his wife Catherine and their three children.
Catherine was mother of John Johnson, Mary Johnson, and
Nancy Johnson. By this period, William Johnson had become
a man of considerable means. He owned a large estate of over
three thousand acres, an area of about two miles square. Over
500 acres were plowed and ready to plant. Johnson had trad-
ed with the local Germans, with members of the Iroquois
Confederation and he had learned the ways of the frontier.
The groundwork seemed to be laid for an excellent future.

CHAPTER 2

The Six Nations

A fter a few years at Mount Johnson, William became a wealthy man. His future was even more promising. Since the remainder of his life would be intertwined with the history of the Six Nations of Iroquois Indians, a basic survey of this powerful group of Native Americans is required before continuing further.

The Iroquois Confederation originally consisted of five nations.

> These were joined together like the United Provinces and without any Superiority of the one over the other. Each of these Nations was an absolute Republic and every Castle in each Nation makes an independent Republick, and was governed in all publick Affairs by its own Sachems or old men[1]

The five nations included "the Mohawks, Oneidas, Onondagas, Cayugas, and Senecas."[2] The sixth nation, the Tuscaroras, joined the organization in about 1710.[3]

The Iroquois, according to Caldwalder Colden ... "strictly followed one maxim, formerly practice by the Romans."[4] They increased their strength by adopting their captives or encouraging their former enemies to incorporate with them.[5] Many times, these other groups of Native Americans:

if they behaved well, became equally esteemed with their own People so that some of their Captives had afterwards become their greatest sachems and captains.[6]

The Iroquois were known for making war but, by controlling a large area of northeastern North America, they also helped to keep the peace. This peace was kept by force when necessary and by diplomacy when possible. This union of American aborigines:

> dominated all surrounding tribes and from their homeland in northern New York between the Hudson and Niagara Rivers maintained a pax iroquoia that in their most heroic days had extended from New England to the Illinois region and from the Ottawa River to Chesapeak Bay.[7]

Legend states that the Iroquois Confederation was started by Deganawidah, a Huron prophet; and Hiawatha. an Onondoga brave, who eventually became a Mohawk. Deganawidah and Hiawatha supposedly spread a message of peace. Finally, the prophet's beliefs were accepted and the five nations joined.[8] This union of the Iroquois began about 1570, according to typical accounts.[9] In actuality, the date may have been much earlier. Historians have various estimates of when the league began. David Cusick, in his fanciful history, places it in 1450.[10] Others place the date between 1600 and 1630.[11]

According to legend, the Iroquois ruled their territory in the years before the Europeans by statesmanship, rather than by force.[12] The Iroquois also punished those who disturbed the peace and yet stressed the need for cooperation and a viable government that could work. This was after the Iroquois took control of the territory of the Algonquins when they first arrived in the New York area.[13] The governmental organization of the Iroquois was admired by not only William Johnson, but by American statesmen such as Benjamin

Franklin and is rumored to have influenced the content of the United States Constitution.

The eastern most tribe of the Iroquois Confederation was the Mohawks who were keepers of the eastern door. Next came the Oneidas, the Onondagas, the Cayugas, and finally the Senecas, who were keepers of the western door. The Tuscaroras, who fled from white penetration in North Carolina, were admitted in 1710 and lived on the territory of the Oneidas.

In their early history the Iroquoian tribes or Nations had, been farmers and hunters. "All the Iroquoians tilled the soil."[14]

> All their usuages were adapted to a land of warm summers and severe winters. Their corn itself was a harder and earlier ripening variety than that of their Delaware neighbors.[15]

The Iroquois ... "had cultivated corn and other crops from a remote period."[16] This was the main way the Iroquois subsisted until contact with the whiteman.

By about 1640, the Iroquois supplied the white man's need or desire for furs. The fur trade changed the Iroquois way of life and led to a series of conquests.

> The position of the Iroquois was equally strong for conquest in all directions. The Ohio and Susquehannah valley led south and west away from their highland, offering easy access to enemy country and making possible the sudden assaults for which the Iroquois became notorious.[17]

The fur trade transformed the Iroquois from an agricultural society to one of hunters and collectors of furs. Before this time ... "the Iroquois, who were led later by the Mohawks, were not conquerors."[18] Realizing that they could be at a distinct "disadvantage in intertribal warfare, they tried ceaselessly to make a permanent arrangement by treaty."[19] Their willingness to negotiate for peaceful solutions to problems with the French in the 1620's is one example.

> On June 2, 1622, Iroquois deputies arrived at Three
> Rivers to arrange a peace with the French, which
> was confirmed after an interval to allow for its ratifi-
> cation in Iroquoia, in 1624. This peace was made
> only with the Mohawks, for the upper nations were
> not yet interested.[20]

Negotiations for peace were not successful in the 1620's
and 1630's. The relationship between the Iroquois and the
Hurons, Algonquins and the French, had been one of trade.[21]
The Five Nations tried repeatedly to establish a peaceful solu-
tion and be able to obtain enough beaver pelts to make a profit for themselves. Peaceful means "were unsuccessful because
of the machinations of the French and the indifference of the
French Indians, some of whom were uncooperative as late as
1645.[22] It thus can be stated that

> until 1641 the Iroquois were far from aggressive; the
> Hurons and Algonquins invaded their country at
> pleasure, and felt carelessly secure in their own
> lands. Between 1640 and 1645 the Iroquois, finding
> it necessary to their own maintenance to acquire
> furs, and discovering that the Huron fur brigades
> were vulnerable, became increasingly aggressive,
> and their ambuscades on the river became so
> numerous and so successful that the French hoped
> for relief through a peace. In the peace arranged in
> 1645 there appears to have been but one provision
> of importance, the one enunciated by Kiotsaeton to
> the Hurons and Algonquins, that both were to come
> to the Iroquois to trade.[23]

During the years after 1645, the Iroquois more and more
became hunters and traders of beaver pelts which were valuable to the English and the French. The Iroquois extended
their power far and wide to obtain these pelts. Thus, after
1645, the Iroquois became much more aggressive. They

became the most warlike people in America, and were a bulwark between the English and their enemies.[24] They went as far as ... "the South Sea the North West passage and Florida to warr."[25] In fact, their power became so considerable, that all the Indians in the northeast paid them tribute.[26]

The Iroquois needed furs to exchange for guns, powder, broadcloth, hoes and axes. These were needed for subsistence and defense.[27] In the year "1640 scarely a beaver was to be found between the Hudson River and the Genesee."[28]

> The Iroquois, to save themselves, had either to find new hunting grounds or to capture a position as middlemen (like the Hurons whose country was also denuded of beaver) in the trade between the white man and the far Indians in the north and west, where the best hunting lay.[29]

The Iroquois thus waged war against those who could improve their position in the fur trade. In 1649, one thousand braves were sent against the Hurons at St. Ignace.[30] A Few Hurons escaped to warn St. Louis; however, it was too late. St. Louis also felt the Iroquois wrath.[31] It went down in flames in March of 1649.[32] The Hurons tried a desperate counterattack which drove the members of the confederation back to their own territory.[33] However, the Iroquois' goal had been met, for the Hurons dispersed in all directions, never again to be a threat to them or to hold their former position in the fur trade.

In turn, other Indian nations were defeated by the Iroquois. The Petuns were overrun in 1649. The Neutrals met a similar fate in 1650-51, as did the Eries in 1654.[34]

The reasons for all this aggression can be summarized in a few words. The Iroquois ..."wage war to secure a good peace."[35] What the Iroquois wanted in all their conquests was a better share of the fur trade.[36] The Iroquois were willing to suffer the consequences of ... "disastrous war, and procure at the same time freedom of trade.[37]

As the years went by, both the English and the French vied for Iroquois trade and support. Each tried to convince the

Indians that the other was not a true friend of the Iroquois and would ultimately seek their destruction. For instance, in September, 1689, Colonel John Pynchon, Major Thomas Savage, Captain Andrew Belsher, and Captain Jonathan Bull, who were agents of several governments of New England, tried to win over the Indians and explain the recent Glorius Revolution in England.[38] Later, the group noted that the French were enemies of the Five Nations. It was stated that:

> So long as ye French king and ye Jesuits have ye Command at Canida you can never Expect to live in Peace it being there only Studdy not only to Dukkoy and Treacherously murther your People butt to Send evill Emissaries amongst you as they did Lately from ye Eastward, to Delude and Raise Jealousies Against your Best Frindes who have kept there Covenant Chain Inviolable time out of minde.[39]

The Iroquois did, on many occasions, help the English of New England. The Mohawks, for instance, stood

> between New England and Canada like a wall of fire against French and Indian attacks, but time and again they helped the settlers to overcome their own Indian neighbors.[40]

Examples of Iroquois' help to New England are numerous. In November and December of 1675, they stopped King Philip's Indians about forty miles from Albany.[41] Later in September, 1689, Tahajadoris, a Mohawk sachem, stated to agents of New England that

> When you had Wars some time ago with the Indians, you desired us to help you; we did it readily; and to the Purpose; for we pursued them closely, by which we prevented the Effusion of much of your Blood[42]

During the late 1600's, the Iroquois, at times, played the English against the French and vice versa when the situation arose. The legend that the Iroquois refused to side at all with the French after Samuel de Champlain's firing on them during the early seventeenth century is only legend. The Iroquois tried to make various treaties with the French, or tried to remain neutral after the Champlain encounter.[43] "The Career of Sir William Johnson shows that the English could not, without extreme exertions, depend on the friendship of the Iroquois or on their being hostile to the French."[44]

During the summer of 1701, what the English had feared for years came true. In Montreal, the Five Nations made peace with the French and their Indian Allies.[45] The French invited the Iroquois to trade at Detroit. In return, the Five Nations agreed to stay neutral in any further conflict between the French and the British.[46] The French also promised to stay out of Iroquois territory.

The French, however, recently thereafter sent diplomats and friendly Indians to persuade the Iroquois to trade with them, and even fight the British. The trade was the main reason for these negotiations. The French and the English played tug of war with the Iroqouis throughout the colonial period.[47] Both nations wanted the five and then six nations to trade with them and abandon the other. For instance, in May of 1711, Monsieur Longville spoke to the Iroquois, for the French. He then "made a Present of near £600—in value mostly Amunition.[48]

The Iroquois reported what Longville said to Colonel Schuyler and other British officials.[49] This is what Longville said;

> That he was come to speak to them in behalf of all the other Nations of Indians in the French Alliance; that all past Evil on each side should now be forgot and forgiven, and that they should now renew the Covenant between them and not listen to any Evil Insinuations to the contrary from the Govr. of New York.
>
> He then proceeded to tell them, that the Govr. of

New York had no other regard for them but on account of their Bever, that he hearkend to none of their Requests. He warned them from taking the Hatchet from the Govr. of New York against the French, to remain Neuter and let the French and English decide their Quarrells with One Another. Threatened them if they did not listen to this Advice it would end in their own Destruction.[50]

Colonel Schuyler replied to the Iroquois by thanking them for telling him of the French visit and informing them the Governor of New York and the Queen of England expected allegiance to the Crown.[51] Furthermore, he stated that in the future "you will not permit any armed Men, Priests, or Emissarys from the French to come amongst you."[52] He continued by stating he also

expects you will have no private Consultations with any of those French who were lately amongst you. And if any Attempt be made upon you from Cannada his Excelly assures you. of all the possible assistance this Govt can give you.[53]

As the French and the British vied for control of the fur trade and also for control of the North American continent, the competition for the support of the Indians became serious business. Adept brokers "well connected to networks of political influence in local communities on both sides of the cultural divide played essential roles in trading partnerships and military alliances."[54] The need for brokers was obviously necessary for both Britain and France.

Without brokers' communication skills and abilities to please diverse interest groups, peoples with vastly differing political structures, economic systems, and cultural beliefs could hardly talk to each other, much less work together. The point is nowhere better illustrated than in relations between the English of New York and the Five Nations of the Confederacy, two of the key players in late seventeenth-century North American diplomacy and warfare.[55]

The use of cultural brokers, or diplomats was continued in the eighteenth century by both Britain and France. The British tried to keep alive the "diplomatic ties among English colonies and Indian peoples known in the language of native diplomacy as the 'Covenant Chain.'"[56] This was difficult to accomplish, for the Iroquois had not benefitted in King William's War by fighting against the French.

> The Iroquois and the English fought, independently but in concert, against New France and its Indian allies in the conflict colonials called King William's War. The experience was an almost unmitigated disaster for the Five Nations, whose English friends provided little assistance. The fighting stopped only after confederacy leaders agreed to French demands that they remain neutral in future conflicts between European empires.[57]

Therefore, during the eighteenth century, the Iroquois were divided in their allegiance toward France and Britain. The western tribes stayed neutral for the most part. The Senecas even sided with the French to a large extent. Only the Mohawks stayed somewhat loyal to the British.[58] This was the situation when William Johnson walked onto the stage of history in colonial New York in 1738. His diplomatic skills were still undeveloped at the time. Before they would surface, the young colonial had to learn to respect and admire his Native American neighbors.

By the year 1745, William Johnson no longer depended on his uncle Peter Warren, and rarely contacted his family. His lack of contact with his brother in Boston is an example of this. The letter dated August 25, 1746 states in part:

> I have wrote Several letters to you since my arrival here but have not Receiv'd an Answer I beg you'l write to me in Boston, and Derect to the Care of Mr Charles Apthorp.[59]

This letter is signed "Yr Most Loveing and Affect Bro. Warren Johnson."[60]

William Johnson lived during an era when communication over long distances was difficult at best. Yet the question remains, why did William not write his brother during the years immediately after moving his family to Mount Johnson? The answer to this question, although somewhat conjectural, is also partially obvious. William was building up his business. His time was undoubtedly taken up in trading mainly with the Six Nations of Indians and with local Germans.

For the colonial New Yorker to later influence the Indians, he needed to learn all he could about their culture. He also had to develop a thorough understanding of the Native Americans. The mutual respect between William Johnson and the natives began soon after he settled in colonial New York. Something in his natural makeup responded to the culture of the aborigines[61] He had copied their ways in order to survive and succeed on the frontier. In fact, according to Milton Hamilton, Johnson, unlike other traders and merchants,

> did not despise the Indians' customs or way of life, and he could live, work, and dress with them as brothers. He learned their language, discovered their forms of social conduct, and their government, and hence learned to work and speak in their terms. This sympathetic understanding of another people is the real basis of diplomacy. Thus, Johnson rose above the role of merchant to that of diplomat and statesman.[62]

William Johnson could have easily treated the Indians unfairly and become rich in the process. He decided not to take part in such practices. Greedy traders and those who hated Native Americans were numerous throughout American colonial history. "It was to the eternal credit of William Johnson that, although surrounded by greedy traders and Indian haters, he developed respect for the Indian and learned to appeal to his better nature."[63]

Johnson put in writing numerous times, his respect and admiration of Native Americans. In a letter to his uncle Peter Warren of July 24, 1749, he discussed his dealing with the Germans and the Indians. He stated:

> I can say without boasting, I have obtained by my far dealing with the German Settlers & ca up [which means and came up]the Mohawks River, who are grown Considerable, and will in time possible be ye majority in the County of Albany, besides my Scituation among the Indians, and integrity to them, made these poor Savages Seek to me, so that I have a Superior Interest with them, which Sort of interest is the most advantagious to this Province.[64]

It is obvious that the famed New Yorker looked on his integrity and fair dealings with the Germans and the Indians as extremely important. Unlike other merchants who traded with the natives, Johnson always thought of the total picture when dealing with them. He did not operate from short sighted visions which pushed him to make a quick profit and then move on. He realized that he wanted to trade with the same Indians over a long period, and thus, had to be fair in order to depend on their continued business. Gradually, the Native Americanss trusted the colonial merchant. If he did not treat them fairly, he would have never obtained their long term trade. William Johnson's policy of trade toward his Native American neighbors was not only fair and just. It reflected sensitivity and proved to be profitable. By the 1740's, the fur trade was big business in colonial New York, and reached proportions as high as five times its former size.[65] Johnson took full advantage of this situation.

William Johnson, like every merchant and trader, needed to make a profit in his trade with the Indians. One way of doing this was to sell rum to Native Americanss, which was a common practice. He was against the Reverend Barclay's attempt to limit the sale of liquor to Indians. Throughout most of his dealings with the Six Nations, he felt that rum would not hurt them. This opinion changed during the French and Indian War period when various sachems complained to Johnson that the "white people selling Rum to the Indians represented the ill consequences thereof and prayed that it may be prevented."[66] He then turned conservative, agreeing that the consequences of such sale were detrimental to the common interest.[67]

Partly because of his liberalness toward his fellow humans, and partly because fair treatment was good business practice, William Johnson developed a deep respect for Native Americans. As William Leete Stone stated in his biography;

> It has already been noted, that it was Mr. Johnson's policy to cultivate an intimate acquaintance with the Indians. Being largely engaged in commerce with them, his facilities to that end were great; and no white man perhaps, ever succeeded in more entirely winning their confidence. He mingled with them freely; joined in their sports; and at pleasure assumed both their costumes and their manners and cast them aside, as circumstances might require. He was consequently fast gaining an ascendency over them upon which the French looked with exceeding jealousy.[68]

As stated, during William Johnson's time, cheating the Indians and extreme prejudice toward them was common. It was common for white traders and settlers to think of their immediate profit, always at the expense of Native Americans. The legendary Robert Rogers, for instance, in his play "Ponteach: or the Savages of America, A Tragedy" states in dialogue between two main characters that ... "our fundamental maxim is this, that it is no crime to cheat and gull an Indian."[69] When Murphy, the young trader in the play protests, McDole, the older more experienced trader, states that the younger must abide by the rule.[70] If this was carried out, the cheating merchant would grow rich. [71]

Cheating the Native Americans was easy to most white merchants. The method was generally to get the Indians drunk.

The alcohol was strengthened by certain drugs, that made the Indians mad.[72] In this irrational state, their furs would soon leave their hands.

> One small slip would turn three pounds to one;
> Which they poor silly souls! Ignorant of weights and
> rules of balancing did not perceive.[73]

Hatred of the aborigines during much of American history was commonplace. This was definitely the case during William Johnson's time and even in the nineteenth century when it was said that a "good Indian was a dead Indian". Even Francis Parkman, the noted historian, felt that the Indians were not different from the forests or wild animals; in the name of civilization, all could be pushed aside or killed off.[74] The Indian, to much of white America, was a menace that had to be eliminated. This idea was prevalent in New England, the deep South, and later in the far west. The Indian, according to this view, was in league with the devil and definitely an adversary.[75] These "savages" were blamed for taking many lives. Some went so far as to state that all difficulties in English colonization and settlement could be directly blamed on the Indian in all parts of colonial America.[76]

Many times white colonials blamed Native Americans for all the problems in the frontier of North America. They blamed them for killing the game in the forests and almost every other problem.

> These hateful Indians kidnap all the Game. Curse
> their black Heads! they fright the Deer and Bear and
> ev'ry animal that haunts the wood or by their witch-
> craft conjure them away. Curs'd Heathen Infidels!
> Mere Savage Beasts. They don't deserve to breathe
> in Christian Air, And they should be hunted down
> like Brutes.[77]

During Johnson's time, a typical white person thought Indians were bloodthirsty savages to be feared and hated and not to be trusted. For an affluent British subject to favor the Native Americans was different at best. It is no wonder that

Johnson suffered criticism from much of white society for his liberal Indian philosophy.

Johnson realized that trade with the Six Nations would make him wealthy. However, he also had a liberal position on race that was rare for his time. He demonstrated this over and over again by befriending many of his native neighbors. He also did not try to hide intimate relationships with at least two Indian women.

The most famous and important Indian woman that William Johnson cohabited with was Mary Brant. Mary had been his housekeeper and replaced Catherine Weisenberg. The date is somewhat conjectural, but may have been April, 1759.[78] It is likely that Catherine died then, although she bore no children after 1742.[79]

> She may have lived on in relative ill health, and served as Sir William's hausfrau, for she was never regarded as "lady" Johnson. Mary Brant then would have succeeded her immediately as housekeeper, and it is in this year that Mary's first child, Peter, the natural son of Sir William, was born. It is in this year too, that the first mention of Mary Brant appears in the Johnson Papers.[80]

It, of course, can be argued that many frontiersmen established intimate relationships with Indian women. It was not always common, but not unheard of in British America. However, it was very uncommon that the children that were the outcome of such a union would be recognized, and furthermore, that they would be provided for in his will. William Johnson's will states in part;

> To Susanna, Daughter of Mary Brant and Sister of the foregoing Six Children, I Devise and bequeath Three thousand Acres of the Royal Grant now called Kingsland to be laid out adjoining to them of her Sister Mary.
>
> To Anne, Sister of the foregoing seven Children by

Mary Brant I Devise and Bequeath Three Thousand Acres of the Royal Grant now called Kingsland, to be laid out next to that of her Sister Susannah, And to be by her and the Heirs of her body lawfully begotten, forever quietly and peaceably possessed and enjoyed.

To Young Brant alias Kaghnechtago of Canojohare I give and bequeath One thousand Acres of Land in the Royal Grant now called Kingsland to be layed out next to and adjoining the before mentioned Land of Anne Daughter of Mary Brant. Also to William alias Tagawirunte of Canajohare, One thousand Acres of Land in said Royal Grant, alias Kingsland, adjoining that of Brants, to be by them and the Heirs of their bodys lawfully begotten forever quietly and peacefully possessed and enjoyed.[81]

The Johnson will goes on to state that all eight children of Mary Brant would be left shares and that if any of them should die without offspring, the real estate left them would be divided among the survivors. It also states that Mary Brant would be left Lot Number One of the Royal Gant Kingsland and two hundred pounds of New York money three months after Johnson's death.[82]

It is somewhat obvious that a man who would provide for his "half-breed" children and his Indian lover was very liberal for eighteenth century America. William Johnson was not at all ashamed of having Indian children and, although he never married their mother, respected and appreciated them. He was, indeed, a rare white man for his time.

Johnson was especially gracious in his treatment of the Mohawks. He spent an enormous amount of time learning their language in order to communicate with them properly. The Mohawk tongue was supposedly so difficult, that even officials from Albany entrusted with Indian affairs rarely were successful with it.

The friendship that William Johnson had with the Mohawks

and with a number of individual Indians, has become legendary. In this instance, the legend was also fact, and can be documented in many sources. For instance, on November 24, 1746, a meeting between Indian commissioners and Mohawk sachems took place

> at which Hendrick and eight other Indians appeared though they had refused to appear at another meeting earlier the same day. They gave as a reason for their non-appearance the fact that they were responsible to Colonel Johnson.[83]

Hendrick was a well known Mohawk Chief and a very close friend to Johnson. The meeting occurred during King George's War when the English were eager to gain Indian allies. Obviously, Hendrick and other Native American leaders befriended and trusted William Johnson above all other British leaders.[84] "They looked upon him as their Chief, their Patron, and their Brother, they acted under his Command and were almost wholly directed by him."[85]

Johnson showed great respect for Hendrick and other sachems. For instance, he wrote to Governor Clinton on February 25, 1747, stating that he needed "Blankets, linnen, paint, Guns, Cutlashes and ca."[86] to fight the French. He also was concerned about Hendrick, who had been sick but was now recovering.[87] Governor Clinton replied on March 25, 1747 that he would write to William Shirley to get the supplies Johnson needed.[88] In the same letter Clinton stated, "I am very Glad to hear my Friend Hendrick is on the recovery and pray let him know I Say so."[89] Undoubtedly, Johnson cared deeply for the old chief as did the Governor. Also, it was obvious to both men that the old Indian's good health would be a great service to the British cause.[90]

Other Indians also indicated their confidence in William Johnson's leadership. Abraham, for one, felt that the New York leader was needed to insure fair and friendly relations with the Six Nations. [91] Both Hendrick and Abraham agreed with Johnson that British forts were needed deep in Iroquois territory to insure British dominance of the French and to persuade far off Indians to become allies.[92]

Although he was most loyal to the Mohawks, who were closest to Mount Johnson geographically, William Johnson had great respect for all of the Six Nations and also other Indians. He respected and understood their culture, their customs, their history, and their ability to live in harmony with nature. He was, in one way, a British official, loyal to the Crown. On the other hand, he was a brother to the Mohawks. In turn, they gave him the Indian name of Warraghigagey, "which signifies A man who undertakes great things."[93]

William Johnson was smart enough to realize that following Indian ways gave him considerable influence over the Mohawks and other Iroquois. This ultimately would help in getting them to fight as allies of Britain.

> When the Indians came to the Town of Albany on the 8th of August (1746), Mr. Johnson put himself at the Head of the Mohawks, dressed and painted after the Manner of an Indian War-Captain; and the Indians that followed him were likewise dressed and painted, as is usual with them when they set out in War.[94]

Therefore, William Johnson's fair treatment and practices with Native Americans set the stage for his future. King William's War in the 1740's was a great test of his Indian policies. Johnson faced this conflict, as he did with his early life, with fortitude and vigor.

CHAPTER 3

Gaining Military Experience

In 1740, Frederick the Great of Prussia, treacherously seized the province of Silesia from Austria. Maria Theresa, the Austrian queen, fought back with vigor. Spain and France sided with Prussia. Britain entered the conflict as an ally of Austria. In Europe, the conflict was known as the War of Austrian Succession and was fought from 1740 to 1748. In America, it was called King George's War and lasted from 1744 to 1748.

When hostilities began, the Indian Commission had recommendations for Governor George Clinton of New York.

> Albany 13 June 1744.
> The Commission wrote to the Governor that as War is now declared between the French and English, they think it absolutely necessary that an outscont of 40 Men should be sent at the charge of the Province (should be sent) to the Carrying place (a Pass between Albany and Crown Point) to observe the Motions of the Enemy and that a Fort or Place of Strength should be built at the said Carrying Place as a Rendevouz or retreat for Out scouts and Partys wch it will be necessary in War time to be continually sending out.[1]

During William Johnson's time, Oswego was a main trading

center for the fur trade. "The English had gained the trade which the French, before that, had with the Indians to the Westward of New York."[2] Indians from many miles away would exchange their pelts for modern commodities.[3]

On their way to trade at Oswego, the Indians would generally pass by Mount Johnson on their way down the Mohawk River. They would take supplies from Johnson's store on credit and pay him on their way back months later.[4] Few traders had faith in the Native Americans that Johnson had.[5] Generally, this trust brought him great profits and, in turn, gained him enormous respect with his Native American brothers. In all the "transactions he acted with so much openness and integrity, that those who once dealt with him thought themselves happy in improving the correspondence.[6]

William Johnson's trading with the natives on their way to Oswego is mentioned because the British control of this site was paramount to the control of the Indian fur trade.[7] The highly prestigious New Yorker had to realize that if Oswego fell to the French, he would lose influence with the Iroquois as well as a great amount of Indian trade. As Peter Wraxall's Indian records stated;

> The Fort at Oswego was the Key of the 6 Nations and that their Fidelity and Allegiance to His Majesty chiefly depends on our supporting the said Fort. Should this place fall into the hands of the French all the Indian Trade of this Colony would go with it, by wth means the French would gain over the 6 Nations and all the other Indians wholly to their Interest.[8]

Therefore, William Johnson, as a trader and merchant went to war not only because he was a British subject, nor because he would lose influence with the Six Nations if the French won, but because if the French took control of sites like Oswego, he would have lost tremendous profits. He had to help defeat the French or at least push them back for his personal gain. His motives in King George's War and later in the French and Indian War were somewhat personal.

Augustus Buell argued that the first years of the war were uneventful for Johnson. He supposedly improved his estate during that period by clearing between two hundred and fifty to three hundred acres a year.[9] According to Buell, "by the end of 1746, he had about 1,200 acres cleared by his own cultivation.[10] He also had hundreds of acres cleared by his tenants which, at the time, numbered about a hundred.[11]

August Buell also discusses that William Johnson bought no slaves during the later part of the war which was about 1747.[12] At this time, he bought an estate in Dutchess County that was sold at administrator's sale in partition.[13]

> This estate included nineteen slaves. Sir William bought the lot entire, though only about ten or eleven of them were able bodied men or women, the rest being aged and infirm, or children.[14]

Augustus Buell was mistaken about Johnson not owning slaves until 1747. A bill of sale dated March 8, 1744, reveals that Johnson owned and traded slaves years earlier. A Negro boy named Stepney was traded to Wessell Vanscoike for a man named Quack, a blacksmith from Albany.[15] Johnson stated that Vanscoike had a right to hold this boy forever.[16] He further defended the "exchange of the above named Negroe Boy against all persons whatever."[17] Thus, it seems that William Johnson owned slaves before 1747.

Dr. Milton Hamilton agrees with this conclusion regarding Johnson's slaves.[18] He also states that slaves were brought to New York from Boston when young William first came to the colony.[19]

Obviously, William Johnson did not extend his liberal views about Native Americans to Africans in bondage. Native Americans helped him learn to survive in the wilderness and, by their trade, made him rich. Africans were of no use to him, except as laborers and servants. His progressive views toward

Native Americans was, therefore, influenced to some extent by profit. This was the case although Buell stated that he built comfortable cabins for the Africans and was a good master.[20]

William Johnson, like many New Yorkers, went about his everyday activities during the early years of the war. He undoubtedly heard of the early events of the confrontation, but was many miles from the action. There was never any serious concern that the French would penetrate as far as the Mohawk valley at that time. However, as noted, Oswego was a possible target that needed to be protected.

During the first period of the war, it was thought that the great trading center may have been safe. In September of 1744, Thomas Butler wrote William Johnson two letters from Oswego, which in part discussed the subject[21] Butler stated on September 16th

> I gave> you some Small acct. of the French being on their way hithr. but find since < it hath been > a false Alarm. I don't now in least susppeckt> that this place will be attacked as < the Five> Nations Seem to have it at Heart.[22]

On September 23rd, Butler wrote again to Johnson concerning goods that the young trader was supposed to send him.[23] He also stated that he thought there would be "no danger from Our Neighbours the French."[24]

Governor George Clinton of New York did not agree with Butler. He believed that Oswego was in grave danger from the French and must not be allowed to fall.[25] He had to find a way to supply the fort and keep it from falling to the French. This would be difficult because the Assembly had provided no funds for the project.[26]

In William Johnson, Governor Clinton found a man who would help Oswego survive against the French. Johnson had a vested interest in the Oswego trade and was becoming influential with the Six Nations. Clinton realized that Johnson's knowledge of the Iroquois culture and language made him the ideal candidate for the job. His first public office had been as Justice of the Peace in his community in 1745.[27]

The reason for Clinton selecting the young trader for this project was also probably influenced by his close association with Chief Justice James DeLancy.[28] William's aunt, Susannah Warren, was originally a DeLancy before she married his uncle, Peter Warren. Judge DeLancy made use of the Governor's confidence to have the positions of importance filled ... "with his relatives or persons dependent on him."[29] His ulterior motives, according to Caldwalder Colden, were devious at best. Colden believed that DeLancy wanted the executive position himself.[30]

It cannot be determined if Caldwalder Colden's evaluation of James DeLancy was correct. In any case, his early association with Governor Clinton was probably the reason why the Governor turned to young Johnson to help Oswego against the French. He undoubtedly also realized that the young trader had a vested interest in keeping Oswego under British control. Eventually, Johnson became a valuable ally to Clinton.[31] His trade was independent of the Dutch in Albany and of the Montreal alliance.[32] Johnson and Clinton had similar interests and were against these powerful groups. Johnson's growing rapport with the Iroquois and knowledge of their language and culture also helped bring the two men together.[33] Governor Clinton's decision to turn to the young Irishmen to help strengthen Oswego and ward off the French was a logical option.

Johnson was put in charge of sending supplies to Oswego and of eventually sending troops. He bought cattle and other supplies from fellow New Yorkers.[34] A letter from Thomas Butler revealed that Butler worked for Johnson by rounding up cattle for the Oswego cause. Butler stated:

> Yesterday I was al over Stone Robie and bought all the Kattle that was good to be found. I have now in all bought thirty Seven. I think very good oxen. Excepting two cows which are about six years old and good. I am now going over the River to one

Countreymans where I hear is two large oxen. The remainder I proposed to buy at the Flatts. I have ordered the people to drive up the Kattle next fryday to Herkemans and think to sett them of ye. Next day for Oswego.[35]

William Johnson was given the right to supply troops to Oswego in the spring of 1746. In a letter to John Catherwood, the young New Yorker stated:

This Inst recd. Yr. favour of the 9th whereby I find the Assembly upon his Excllys recommendation have agreed that I shall Supply the troops at Oswego, wh I will take Care shall be well done, and in due time I intend to sett them of the latter end of this present week, wh is very expeditious, considering the little notice I have had. Please to return my hearty thanks to his Excelly. for the kind favour done me as I shall also in a letter to him.[36]

Johnson felt it an honor that the governor allowed him to supply Oswego. This was evident from the letter just cited. It is also obvious that by April, 1746, Johnson was enjoying a good relationship with the chief executive. Payment for his services was another matter. In a letter to Clinton in October, 1748, Johnson revealed he still had not received payment over two and a half years after the action.[37] Johnson stated:

I have agreable to you Excellcy. orders Sent the Provisions and Relief to Oswego, which as it was Unexpected, put me to a good deal of Difficulty and needless Expense. yet should not so much mind that, could I but get my money regularly payed, which the Province is Justly indebted to me.[38]

Johnson, in the same letter which mentioned lack of payment, sent the governor two black horses and stated that he would soon be making a trip to New York City.[39] It is obvious that his relationship with the chief executive was beyond mere economic endeavors. He was on very friendly terms with Clinton and this made his entrance into public life much easier.

In August of 1746, William Johnson attended an Indian council at Albany.[40] At this council, he was authorized to supply Indian war parties against the French. He was given the title of Colonel of the warriors of the Six Nations of Iroquois and also of white volunteers.[41] By this period, the young trader had "by kindness and tact, obtained almost complete control of the warlike Iroquois."[42] Governor Clinton saw in young Johnson a valuable ally who exercised control and influence over the Native Americans. He also must have realized the great level of integrity that William Johnson possessed.[43]

The honesty and sincerity which the young Irishmen revealed made him a "natural" when dealing with the Indians. His adaptability was also a valuable asset:

> 'He was at ease whether entertaining in his baronial mansion on the Mohawk the polished scion of mobility, or the rude savage; whether mingleing in the salons of wealth and fashion, or seated on the earthy floor of a bark wigwam. The same facility of action was shown in all his varied relations.[44]

The Iroquois, it must be remembered, had stayed generally neutral in affairs between France and Britain since the early 1700's. This was before William Johnson entered on the stage of history. Under the Irishman's influence, the Iroquois began to lean toward the British. This is especially true of the Mohawks during the last two colonial wars and this is evident from a letter Johnson sent to George Clinton on June 23, 1745.[45] Johnson stated:

> I am heartily glad I can send you so good an account of our Indians at the Mohawk Castle, yesterday I went there and called them all together and told them how forward the expedition was at Cape Briton and would be so here likewise in as short time wherefore told them I hoped they would be as ready as well wh. would be the only way of recom-

mending themselves to the favors of ye. Government and all their Brothers here and a great deal more too tedious to mention. Their answer to me was that they would all as one man join heart and hand to fight with us against the french our Common Enemy when ever called upon which I returned them my hearty thanks and gave them a fine large Bull of 5 years old Bread and Liquor equivalent wh. I think they deserved I never saw them behave so chearful before upon any occasion they are to meet and receive the interpreter all painted feathered and dressed.[46]

Johnson was prepared for battle through mobilizing an Indian army to fight the French. However, the winter of 1746-47 was uneventful.[47] By March, warlike activities were beginning to increase. Johnson predicted that his Indians would take many French scalps and burn many settlements.[48] This did occur as the famed New Yorker sent out war parties to ambush the French whenever he could. The war was generally not fought in large battles, but in small skirmishes which attempted to destroy New France's will to fight. For instance, on April 24, 1747, Johnson sent a party of Indians commanded by Lieutenant Walter Butler to Crown Point.[49] A number of the enemy were killed and three were wounded during this confrontation.[50] The enemy retreated and most of their party escaped. Johnson later wrote to Governor Clinton, ... "our Indians inraged fought more like Devils than Men."[51]

Throughout this period, young William who, after August 26, 1748, was Colonel Johnson, became more and more involved in the war effort. However Colonel Johnson, the Mohawk leader and war chief, was still William Johnson the trader and merchant.[52] He sold supplies from his store for the war effort. "Our more scrupulous age calls this graft; but the easy morality of the eighteenth century saw no harm in such a combination of interests."[53] The Johnson store was a busy place.[54] The young merchant fought for the British crown and influenced the Iroquois to do the same. He also made out-

standing profits because of the war, like many capitalist entre-
preneurs in later wars.

King George's War had taken many turns. When the news of
war had arrived in the colonies in 1744, the English fishing sta-
tion at Canseau was taken by a force from Louisbourg. Later
that year, and in 1745, the French and their Indian allies tried
to take Annapolis.[55] Three attempts were unsuccessful.
"Reinforcements and supplies though the men were very
imperfectly armed – arrived in time from Massachusetts,
while the assistance expected by sea for the French did not
appear in time."[56]

The strength of the French forces was an obvious threat to
British colonies in New England. Louisbourg was a menace to
all New England towns. Governor William Shirley of
Massachusetts was concerned when hostilities began and
wrote to Peter Warren concerning the matter.[57] It was eventually decided that an attack on Louisbourg would be undertak-
en. William Pepperell led the land forces from New England,
assisted by Warren, who commanded a naval assault on the
French center.[58] The maneuver was a complete success, and
Louisbourg fell on June 16, 1745.

The conquest of Louisbourg, according to Caldwalder
Colden, was a much more difficult task than any attempted in
Canada. He believed this because no Indians were used during
the attack.[59] Louisbourg marked the only major venture in
North America by the British during the war, although other
ventures were planned and will be discussed later.

Meanwhile, in New York, the French were beginning to rav-
age the countryside and many settlers of the Mohawk valley
moved to Albany to be in safer surroundings. This was the
case, although "the French Indians (also) brought their plun-
der often to Albany."[60] At the time, French danger from the
west threatened the Mohawk Valley and also the New England
area to the northeast.

William Johnson, like many of his neighbors, was advised to
move to Albany. He was told in a letter dated November 26,
1745 from James Wilson, that a room was available for him

and also one for his immediate servants. The letter reveals that William's life was in danger by late 1745. It states that Johnson should

> Live here (Albany) this winter Till These Troublesome Times is a Little [ ] have kept a Room a propus for you and they beg that you would Send Down the best of your Things Directly and there is Room anouf for your Servants. If you will bring them Down I would not have you to stay there for the french have told our Indians that they will have you Dead or alive.[61]

A few days after this letter from James Wilson, William Johnson received a letter from Robert Sanders stating that the French had attacked Saratoga and burned many houses.[62] This occurred on the 17th of November 1745, according to the correspondence.[63]

> At Break of day or > an hour or two Before Day a Number of 400 French <& 220> Indians appeared and did Besett all the houses there, <Burnt &> Destroyed all that Came before them left only one Sawmill Standing wch. stood a Little out their way it seems, took along with them such Booty as they thought fit, Kilt and took Captives 100 or 101 persons Black and white The Unfortunate Capt. Philip Schuyler was Kilt.[64]

It is obvious that the New York frontier was a dangerous place by late 1745 and 1746. Augustus Buell in his biography of Sir William Johnson, portrayed the early years of King George's war were uneventful for William Johnson and that he cleared land and carried out everyday activities. In actuality, although everyday activities occurred, William Johnson fortified his home for war and did his best to continue the war effort. He did not seek safe shelter as advised. This seemed to be against his principles. If there was to be fighting, he would participate. The French never did attack his farm or store,

41

although the threat was certainly evident during those turbu-
lent times. Peter Wraxall's Indian record revealed the kind of
danger that hardy New Yorkers faced.

> 22 April 1746.
> The Commissrs receive an Acct. and transmit it to
> the Govr. of the Barbarous Murder and Scalping of a
> principal Farmer at Schaahkook by the French
> Indians wch they say will drive away all the Settlers
> from their Farms to the Northward of Albany and
> the Westward of Schenectady and down the Eastern
> side of Hudson's River.[65]

As the war continued, William Johnson's destiny was taking
shape. Governor George Clinton trusted the young Irishmen
and the young merchant – frontiersman responded. Clinton
distrusted the Indian commissioners and Philip Livington, the
Secretary of Indian Affairs. In the spring of 1746, Clinton sent
William Johnson among the Mohawks.[66] Johnson's official
authority over the Iroquois Confederacy thus began. Three
years later, on August 2, 1749, he sent the young Indian agent
all the papers from the Department of Indian Affairs.[67]

On August 19, 1746, Governor George Clinton spoke in
Albany by using an interpreter to members of the Six Nations
and river Indians to try to convince them to fight the French
in the upcoming planned conquest of Canada. He put the
hatchet of war against the French in their hands.[68] He remind-
ed them of:

> their Promise to use it againsy the French if they
> made any Attacks and Committed any Hostilities
> upon their Bretheren the English – he told them
> they are all Witnesses of the Bloody and
> Treacherous Murders committed by the French and
> their Indians and he therefore demanded from them
> the imediate fulfilling of their Engagements.
> He acquainted them with the intended Expedition
> against Canada and Levies raised for the same. He
> invited them to share the honour and Glory of this

expedition and presented to them the Great War belt.[69]

William Johnson attended the meeting in Albany on August, 1746. He had come with the Mohawks and was dressed and "painted after their manner."[70] He had the honor of a sachem conferred upon him at this conference and his influence among the Mohawks was very great.[71]

James Thomas Flexner, in his biography, stated that Johnson was adopted as a Mohawk and made a blood brother.[72] There is no evidence in the *Sir William Johnson Papers* and other primary documents that this was factual. The respect the Mohawks had for Johnson was mistaken by Flexner to mean he went through some official ceremony. Flexner was in error with this conclusion.

Milton W. Hamilton felt that William Johnson, like all Indian diplomats and those Governors, that wanted to influence the Indians, dressed and acted in this manner.[73] He stated the Joncaires, the famous French diplomats of the Indians, did the same, as did many others.[74] "Johnson wore many hats and this was only one aspect of his versatility."[75]

The fall of Louisbourg in June of 1745 made a much larger conquest by the British very probable. William Shirley visited with William Pepperrell and Peter Warren after Louisbourg fell to discuss this possibility.[76] Eventually, the Duke of Newcastle issued a circular that directed all governors of the British colonies to raise as many men as possible to attack the three main strongholds of New France.

New England troops were to proceed to Louisbourg to join up with landed naval forces from England.[77] These forces were to attack Quebec; this was the first part of the plan.

Meanwhile, all the other colonies, including New York, were to combine with as many Iroquois Nations as possible and meet at Albany.[78] This large force was to level Crown Point and then Montreal.

William Johnson got as many Mohawks and other Indians as possible ready to march toward Crown Point. The plan, according to Caldwalter Colden, had over two thousand

Indians involved in the expedition.[79] About one thousand were to be sent in small groups to spread out and cause confusion in the surrounding country.[80] Another one thousand were "to go along with the Forces to scour the woods and prevent surprises or falling into Ambuscades."[81]

William Johnson himself originally was not supposed to march to the final destination at Crown Point. This was stated in a letter to Johnson from George Clinton dated August 28, 1746, one year before the expedition began.[82] Governor Clinton stated;

> Whereas I am of Opinion that your residence among the Mohawks, will rather promote his Majestys Service, than if you was to go out with any Command Your self, You are therefore hereby required to reside near the Indian Castles in order to send out the Several Partys as aforesaid, and receive them, at their Return, and to give me Intelligence from time to time of what they have done and of what further Encouragement You shall think necessary for the Service.[83]

In the same letter, Governor George Clinton gave William Johnson general instructions on how to run the expedition of Indians.[84] The governor, while trusting Johnson, was also keeping a fairly tight grasp on what was to occur. As Clinton stated;

> 1st
> You are hereby impowred to inlist Your Command all such Christains and Indians as shall Voluntarily offer themselves for the above mentioned Service, and such Christains as enter into said Service, shall be allowed and paid after the rate of two Shillings New York Currency a Day.
>
> 2dly
> You are to endeavour and send out as many Party's of the said Indians as you possibly can against the

French and their Indians in Canada to harass and Alarm their Quarters in all Parts and to take Prisoners for Intelligence as soon as may be, likewise scalps.

3dly
You will receive with these Instructions, a Number of Blank Commissions in order to appoint such Persons, as You shall think proper to Intrust with any Command.

4thly
In Case you find it Necessary upon any Misbehaviour, or disobedience of the said Officers, to Your Command, to remove him or them for so disobeying, You are hereby, for the good of the Service.[85]

Johnson eventually had about three hundred Indians with him[86] in his March to Crown Point on August 18, 1747.[87] This number disagrees with Caldwalder Colden's account. However, the small parties that were sent out in 1746-47 probably numbered close to the number Colden chronicled.

Johnson and his Mohawks were away from Mount Johnson less than two weeks. They returned to the Johnson home on about September 10th.[88] The reason they returned was that the plan to attack Crown Point was abandoned. The Orders of Governors Shirley and Knowles stated:

His Grace The Duke of Newcastle having in his Letter to Governor Shirley signified That His Majesty finding it necessary to employ the greatest part of his Forces to assist his Allies and defend the Libertys of Europe had thought proper for the present to lay aside the prosecution of the intended Expedition against Canada, and commanded him and Governour Knowles to discharge all the Forces raised for that Service. [89]

Governor Clinton wrote William on September 14, 1747,

four days after his return from Crown Point.[90] He thanked him for his efforts and told him he supported his Indian warfare against the French.[91] Clinton also instructed Johnson to do his best to keep the Indians quiet.[92] The Mohawks that had marched with Johnson were disappointed that no major fighting had occurred. Again, the young leader's ability to influence the Indians and explain to them the situation, was necessary.

For the remainder of King George's War, William Johnson did whatever he could to keep the Mohawks and other Indians neutral or on the side of the British. He also put his case concerning Indian allies directly to the Governor's Council in New York in October, 1747.[93] From October 3-9, Johnson was examined by the council.[94] He was supported strongly by Governor Clinton, who would eventually depend on Johnson for all decisions concerning the Indians.

At the Council, young William Johnson carried himself very well. He recommended the liberal treatment of the Iroquois and, that two forts be built in their area.[95] It was obvious to William and to the council that treating the Indians fairly and providing them supplies and protection would keep them away from French influence.

In his campaign to convince non-believers about the importance of Indian relations, Governor Clinton wrote many letters supporting his fellow Irishmen. On September 27, Clinton wrote the Lords of Trade promoting Johnson's view on Indian warfare.[96] In a letter to the Duke of Newcastle, Clinton favored Johnson's endeavors.[97] In a letter from the governor to the Assembly of October 13, 1747, Johnson's views on Indians were discussed.[98]

To insure that the Six Nations would not be influenced to go to the French side, Johnson was ordered by Clinton to meet with their representatives at Onondaga. On April 11, William left Mount Johnson for Onondaga. [99] The council was held from April 24-26, 1748.[100] The British felt it necessary to keep the Indians away from Canada and the influence of the French. Indians had been captured and the Iroquois wanted to go to

Canada to free them. The British were afraid the French in Canada would influence the Indians to their side.

At Onondaga, young William argued before the Iroquois assembled there that the French and their allies, the Cachewagees, were their enemies.[101] He further stated that both Governor Clinton of New York and Governor Shirley of Massachusetts wanted them not to go to Canada, but to stay home.[102] Johnson continued by stating:

> That the King your Father has sent orders to the Governour to take care of your Castles and Familys while Your Men are out at War And has ordered me to look out proper places to erect Forts for your Safety which I have done since came up here and will immediately set about building them provided you will agree to it, and come together, I have also one thing further to tell you Brethren That the King your Father has sent you a parcel of Goods for the use of Your Families as a Token of his Love to all those who are Hearty in his Cause and mind this News.[103]

The Onondaga conference was a huge success. The Iroquois did not go to Canada although they complained that many of their captives were held by the French.[104] They stated to Johnson ... "had you got them from thence as you have your own People we should not think of going to Canada."[105]

The Iroquois were disappointed by the British program of prisoner exchange. Although some French prisoners were exchanged for native captives, it was not until 1750 that almost all the prisoners were returned to colonial New York. Johnson did his best to get Indian captives returned. He complained to Clinton about the delay in a letter on January 22, 1749.[106] He also stated that if the Indian prisoners were not returned, it was beyond his power to stop the Mohawks from going to get them themselves.[107]

In the end, Iroquois Nations made their own peace with the French. The final official peace that ended the war came on

October 18, 1748, with the Treaty of Aix-la-Chapelle. This resulted in a return to the status quo that had existed before the hostilities started. Thus, Louisbourg was returned to the French.

King George's War, in many ways helped William Johnson. His status changed from a local merchant and trader, to a public figure. He was recognized, by 1748, as the most influential man among the Iroquois Nations. Governors Clinton and Shirley recognized his expertise in this area. He was able to do what was previously thought to be nearly impossible. The Iroquois had remained neutral since approximately 1701 in matters concerning the French and the British. On some occasions, this was not the case, but generally the Iroquois could not be counted on. On July 23, 1746, the Indian commissioners warned Governor Clinton the Iroquois were unwilling to join the war effort against the French.[108] Yet only months later, Mohawks and other Nations were sending war parties against New France. In less than a year, under Johnson's influence, the Mohawks were a viable military force.

CHAPTER 4

Influencing the Mohawks, Other Iroquois Nations, and Indians in General

William Johnson began influencing the Iroquois and other Indians soon after he settled in the Mohawk valley. The integrity he revealed when trading with them resulted in a rapport that was truly remarkable.[1] This relationship and trust between the young Irishman and the Native Americans helped Johnson to develop his business.

During King George's War, it had been assumed that the Iroquois Nations would remain neutral.[2] According to the Indian commissioners, the viciousness of the French would keep them out of King George's War.[3] However, this was not the case. William Johnson turned the Mohawks into a viable ally. When peace resulted in 1748 between Britain and France, Johnson had emerged as the leading diplomat among the Indians. He continued in this endeavor for the remainder of his life.

For his service to the British Crown during King George's War, William Johnson was paid by a Bill of Exchange dated November 5th, 1748, shortly after hostilities ceased. He was paid over two thousand, eight hundred pounds,[4] The letter from Governor George Clinton also revealed the impact the young merchant had on the Iroquois Nations during the previous conflict. Clinton stated;

> To pay unto William Johnson Esqr. or Order the Sum of Two thousand Eight hundred and Thirty Six Pounds thirteen Shillings and one penny ———— Sterling for Value Received of him being upon Account of Sunday Charges incurred in His Majesty's Service for Keeping the Six Nations of Indians and their Allies Strictly Attached to the King's Interest and Steady in their Alliance pursuant to his Majesties Directions Signified to Governour Shirley and me by his Grace the Duke of Newcastle in Letters to us dated the 3d and 27th October 1747.[5]

At this point, Johnson's commission in dealing with the Indians was rewarded by the New York government. His expertise was known to officials in high places. His influence was so great according to Cadwalder Colden, the noted physician, author, and politician, that French effort at persuasion only turned a few Indians against the British.[6] Colden disclosed these facts and the necessity and importance of Indian affairs in a letter to Governor William Shirley on July 25, 1749.[7] He stated that, "Indian affairs deserve the most serious attention as not only a very considerable branch of the British Commerce, but likewise the Security of the Colonies in North America depends upon it."[8]

Colden's letter revealed the considerable influence William Johnson had developed among the Indians by 1749 and the growing respect he had acquired from top officials at this time. The letter states in part;

> The Govr of Canada has at this time sent out a considerable force with a view it is thought to chastise those nations who favour'd us in the late War and to obstruct the English commerce to the Westward. He sent the Caknuagas among the five Nations to incite them to make Wars on the Flatt head and they

would have gon if Coll Johnson had not prevented it. By the information the Govr has from Oswego The Govr of Canada has not been able to persuade any one Nation of Indians to join with him no not so much as the Caknuagas who live near Montreal and were ingaged with him in the last War. Only six single Indians are now gone with the French party.[9]

William Johnson's ability to persuade the Indians to side with the British was, therefore, well known by 1749[10] However, with the war over, he realized that many top officials were not his friends. His success during King George's War with the Indians had made him a number of enemies. Some were obviously jealous of how much the young New Yorker had accomplished during the previous conflict. Others probably disliked Johnson because of his relationship with Governor George Clinton.

With the hostilities over, William Johnson once again thought of his own affairs. He started a new stone house on his property in April of 1749.[11] The Johnson family moved into the new dwelling in January of 1750.[12] The house was surrounded by a palisade five years later, and took the name of Fort Johnson.[13]

William soon realized that his influence over the Iroquois and other Indians did not necessarily make him popular. When he assumed responsibility for the Indians in 1746, he had angered "the Indian commissioners, whom he succeeded, and Philip Livington, who was removed as Indian secretary."[14] Johnson, to these men, was Governor Clinton's man. The rift that was spreading between Clinton and chief justice DeLancey made them disfavor Johnson. After the war, the New York Assembly refused to pay Johnson legitimate amounts incurred as Indian expenses. It, thus, became nearly impossible for him to carry out his work of influencing the Indians without government support.

In July, 1749, Johnson went to New York City to make his own appeal to the colonial government and to the chief justice.[15] He thought that he could convince them to pay him what he was owed by appearing in person. As he stated;

> I have been as Cautious in my Conduct with the dis-
> contented as I possibly Could; they are realy the
> Majority in our Assembly, and I believe are so in all
> Assemblys upon the Continent and naturally averse
> as I find to anything their governours do. I haveing
> acted by Govr. Clintons orders may be in a great
> measure the occasion of their Delay of payment. I
> have now been 12 Days in town, the Assembly
> Sitting, in order to Sollicitte My Demands; the Chief
> Justice I have [not] Seen [as yet, tho I constantly
> frequent the Coffee House he uses Morning and
> Night] once Since I came to town, but Could not find
> him inclined to do me any Service, or even take
> much notice of me wh Surprises me much as I never
> disobliged him, or any of the family. I am sorry to
> say he is the Primum Mobile of the Opposition.[16]

The Assembly did not act on Johnson's request for wages. William must have felt betrayed. The lack of understanding of his value and expenses during peace time in dealing with the Native Americans must have been frustrating. Johnson surely did not want to get involved in a political tug of war. He simply believed that his services concerning the Indians was neces-sary and should be maintained. As he stated concerning this

> My Scituation among the Indians, and integrity to
> them, made those poor Savages Seek to me, so that
> I have a Superior Interest with them, which Sort of
> Interest is the most advantagious to this Province,
> and to all the Neighbouring, and requires their
> Cheifest Policy to Cultivate and Maintain. It is that
> Interest with ye Indians that makes, our Neighbors
> the French an over match as we have woefully
> Known this War.[17]

As a result of this lack of support, William's Uncle Peter Warren suggested that he renounce public business and attend to his own private affairs.[18] If the assembly did not appreciate his real worth, why should he extend himself at his own expense.[19] The tragedy of the situation was that if Johnson left the position of Indian agent, Indian affairs would degenerate to the level they had been when the Commissioners were in power.[20]

The years of 1750 and 1751 passed without special events in the life of William Johnson. His influence with the Indians continued but declined. He did confer with the Mohawk leaders at least twice during that time.[21] As stated earlier, he worked on his estate and finished a new house during this period. He also petitioned for a license to purchase 130,000 acres on the Charlott River, and later bought land around Onondaga Lake.[22] It is probable that by the age of thirty-six, William Johnson had become an extremely wealthy man.

On June 18, 1751, Johnson went to New York again[23] According to Augustus Buell, he went there to submit a list of expenditures to the Committee of Supply in the Assembly.[24] The Governor approved the amounts of £5,700 and £4,276, but the Assembly only approved the first amount.[25] The second amount was forwarded for debate. "Severe animadversions were made upon the close corporations that was alleged to exist between the Governor, Chief-Justice DeLancey, the Attorney-General, and Sir William."[26]

Buell states further that a member of the Assembly, a Mr. Hardenburgh, stated that Johnson had, for years, been Superintendent of Indians and an Indian trader on a large scale. This accusation insinuated graft on the part of Johnson:

> After hearing this Sir William left the hall of the Assembly, and the same afternoon sent a note to Mr. Hardenburgh asking him if he intended by those remarks to impugn his personal integrity. Mr. Hardenburgh promptly replied by inquiring whether he intended his note as preliminary to a demand for satisfaction.[27]

According to the account, the famed New Yorker answered

by stating he intended no duel and only used bullets against his enemies. Thus, he denounced the practice of dueling, which was very common in his day. He also stated that if his integrity was questioned, he would simply open up his books to close examination.[28]

Buell's story is not mentioned by contemporary Johnson biographers such as James Flexner and Milton Hamilton. William had sided with Governor Clinton against Chief Justice DeLancey and, as stated earlier, considered the latter on the opposite side. Also, the Johnson Papers do not contain any mention of this episode in Johnson's life. Therefore, it seems unlikely that such an incident ever occurred at all. It cannot be determined where Augustus Buell got his information.

The truth seems to be that William Johnson was not paid completely for the expenditures concerning the Indians. As a result, he resigned as Indian agent and manager of Indian Affairs on July 5, 1751.[29] The reason for his decision, are as follows:

> It was impossible for him to continue any longer in the Management of Indian Affairs, without a very great detriment, if not ruin, to him in his private Fortune, as well as a very great fatigue to his person. For that before the third day of November 1748, he had (of his private Fortune) advanced in the Management of Indian Affairs, and for the Supply of the Garrison at Oswego, after Others had declined supplying it, because of the War, to the Value of £7177.3. 2 3/4 of which the accounts had been from time duely sworn to by him, and delivered into the Assembly but they only made provision for the payment of £5801.7.4. thereof, so that there remains £1375.15. 10 3/4 without any provision as yet made by the Assembly for the payment thereof, that he has never heard of any Objection made by the Assembly to his Accounts, nor of any reasons why the Assembly have from time to time

delayed the makeing provision for the payment of the said £1375.[30]

At the Council at Albany, at which Johnson gave reasons for resigning as agent and manager of the Six Nations, Governor Clinton and representatives of the Six Nations were in attendance. Also present were Cadwalder Colden, James Alexander, James DeLancey and Edward Holland.[31] The purpose of the Iroquois Nations attending the meeting was to inform the governor of their reaction to Johnson's resignation. The Indians were obviously upset and felt betrayed by the provincial government because of the situation. Henrick spoke for the Iroquois.

> We were very much shocked when Coll. Johnson sent a Belt of Wampum through the Six Nations, to inform us that he declined acting any more with us, and it was the more Terrible, because he was well acquainted with our publick Affairs. We had in War time when he was Like a Tree, that grew for our use, which now seems to be falling down, tho it has many roots; his knowledge of our affairs made us think him one of us (an Indian) and we are greatly afraid, as he has declined, your Excellency will appoint some person, a stranger both to us and our Affairs; and we give your Excellency this Belt of Wampum in order to raise up the falling tree.[32]

The Iroquois wanted Governor Clinton to reinstate Johnson. If he wouldn't, they stated, "we expect to be ruined."[33] Johnson's respect and trust among the Six Nations was at a very high level in July, 1751.

William Johnson was not reinstated at this time because he absolutely refused to continue.[34] He did promise the governor that he would assist him with any advice needed on the Iroquois Nations or other Indians. This response made Clinton look elsewhere for an agent and manager of the Iroquois.

Johnson had suggested John Henry Lydius to take over his

post. Cadwalder Colden stated that he doubted that Lydius would be equal to the task.[35] In their biographies, both James Flexner[36] and Milton Hamilton[37] looked at Lydius as a rival of Johnson and an unscrupulous character. Augustus Buell does not make mention of Lydius.

The reasons that Johnson recommended Lydius are conjectural at best. Perhaps Johnson felt that his personal endeavors had to take precedence over managing the Indians and, before he left that post, had to find a replacement. Johnson stated in a letter to Clinton that "Lydius (if I may be allowed to know the Man, and the disposition of the Indians att present) is the fittest in Albany for a Commissioner."[38]

In the end, no replacement for William Johnson was made. Johnson continued his relationship with the Iroquois Nations and other Indians as he had earlier without his previous title. The Governor made him a member of his Provincial Council on July 10, 1751, only five days after he resigned the office of Manager of Indian Affairs.[39] This insured that he would still take part in public affairs and would have influence on the Indians indirectly.

After 1751, Johnson still found people looking to him for guidance and advice concerning the Iroquois and other Indians. His influence had been so great up to that point that people thought of him as managing the Iroquois Nations, even though officially, he had given up the post. He was looked upon as an overseer of the Mohawk region and as the most influential man with the Iroquois. A letter from James Gimmel dated December 21, 1751, over four months after his resignation, reveals this feeling. It stated:

> Very wise and Prudent Colonel
> Sir:
> Knowing the great vigilance with which you watch over our country, I have deemed it my duty to inform the Colonel without delay that there are some French Indians who wish to settle near or at Oneida Lake, as I was told by a certain Indian. (They

are Frenchmen and not only Indian.) One is well known to your Honor, namely Aquad; odd; and others also. This is all I have to say. Your Honor in his wisdom will know best what to do in this matter.[40]

This letter was written in German and later translated. It gives a microscopic glimpse of how the many German settlers in his region respected William Johnson as their leader and protector against the French and their Indian allies.

From the years 1749 to 1754, relative peace existed between Britain and France. After July, 1751, William Johnson's life was calm compared to the years during King George's War. The years 1751 and 1752 passed without incident. This was to be the calm before the storm.

In 1752, William heard the sad news of his uncle Peter Warren's death in Dublin, Ireland, that past July.[41] Warren Johnson, William's brother, was with Admiral Warren at the time of his death.[42] The elder man suffered "a most Violent Fever which Carried him off in four days."[43]

The year 1753 was more eventful for William Johnson. He began to meet with the Indians again and to influence them. From July 12-16, 1751, he attended a conference with the Mohawks in New York City.[44] From July 26-27, he met with the Mohawks at Mount Johnson.[45] In September, he held a conference with the Six Nations at Onondaga.[46] Although he held no official position in the management of Indian affairs, by 1753, William Johnson was again acting in that capacity.

During 1753, Johnson demonstrated his capacity to entertain noted personalities. Mount Johnson welcomed the best of white society as well as the natives of the frontier. On May 25th, he entertained the Reverend Gideon Hawley.[47]

As Hawley later wrote;

On Friday we left Albany. Mr. Woodbridge and I set out for Mount Johnson, about thirty-six miles off, on the Mohawk river, to pay our compliments to Colonel Johnson, and obtain his countenance in favor of our mission. At sun-set we were politely received at Colonel Johnson's gate, by himself in person. Here we lodged. His mansion was stately, and situate a little distance from the river, on rising ground, and adjacent to a stream which turned his mill. This gentleman was well known in his civil, military, and private character.[48]

In 1753, Johnson also entertained Conrad Weiser. Weiser, a trader in the Ohio valley from Pennsylvania, secured the backing of the Indians of the area. Weiser was a rival of Johnson's in dealing with Indian affairs. Nevertheless, Johnson still welcomed him with kindness and instructed him to visit again any time he was in the Mohawk valley. He also stated Weiser could depend on him to help the Province of Pennsylvania in any affairs dealing with the Indians.[49] However, it was obvious to Weiser that Johnson did not want his company on an upcoming journey to Onondaga in September, during which a conference with the Iroquois Nations was to be held.[50]

Far away from the Mohawk Valley, events were leading to the final conflict between France and Britain. These had begun shortly after peace was declared at Aix-la Chapelle in 1748. The Ohio region was of great interest to the British. Traders from Pennsylvania, such as George Croghan and Conrad Weiser who rapidly expanded their posts in the area. The Virginians were equally interested in the region. They organized the Ohio Company in 1748 and sent out Christopher Gist to explore the region. As a result, a trading house was erected at what is presently Cumberland, Maryland.

The French responded quickly to British expansion by fortifying what is presently Toronto, and diverted trade away from Oswego to a post at Niagara. They also strengthened Detroit and sent out Cèloron de Beinville to seize the Ohio valley in 1749. In the summer of 1752, the trading post of Pickawillany was attacked, and all its defenders were killed.[51]

Thus, the French quickly fortified their territory. They erected Fort Presque Isle, Fort Boeuf, and Fort Venango. Lt. Governor Robert Dinwiddie of Virginia sent young George

Washington to protest these moves. Washington, who at the time was only twenty-one years old, later reported that the French planned to occupy the entire Ohio valley. The only way to remove them was by using force.

In 1754, the hostilities of the last colonial war began. In February, Dinwiddie ordered a fort to be built at the junction of the Allegheny and Monongahela rivers. However, the French seized the site and built Fort Duquesne there. George Washington, who was dispatched with approximately one-hundred and fifty men to occupy the new British fort, built Fort Necessity and resisted a much superior French force. Finally, he had to capitulate to the French leader, Coulon de Villiers on July 3rd.

William Johnson learned of Washington's defeat in a letter dated July 23, 1754. It stated:

> After a Passage of 4 days and a half we arrived here the 16th all in good Health: Since which we have had an Account of Major Washington's Defeat. the inclosed is the News as we have it, tho' very imper-fect. I can hardly credit that part of it, which says, our own Indians fought agst. us. There is no Advice of the Affair from Mr. Dinwiddie, but an Express is daily expected with it. I dare say when we hear the truth it will appear unfavourable enough on our side. It would be some consolation to us under this Loss, might we depend on its raising in the Colonies a proper Resentment, and put them upon raising Supplies of Men and Money, but I fear this is rather to be wish'd for than expected. A French Deserter who left them after they took the Fort at Monongahela, says they had only 500 Men at that time, but before the Season was over expected 4,000.[52]

The preceding letter made it obvious that the writer, Goldsbrow Banyar not only wanted William to know of Washington's defeat, but also of the growing French threat that existed by July of 1754. Also, mentioning that their Indian Allies fought against them[53] made William Johnson realize that his diplomatic services among the Indians were again very necessary.

On June 14, 1754, orders came down from the British government that requested a great congress be held at Albany to unite the colonies against New France.[54] Delegates from seven of the thirteen colonies put in an appearance. These included New York, New Hampshire, Rhode Island, Connecticut, New Jersey, Pennsylvania and Maryland.[55] The southern colonies of Virginia, Georgia and the Carolinas were not represented. They had the war at their back door and were pre-occupied.[56]

Messengers were dispatched to the Iroquois Indian castles to request their attendance at Albany.[57] A secondary purpose of the conference was to keep the powerful Iroquois Confederation on the side of the British in the upcoming war. The Crown realized the value of keeping the Six Nations away from French influence if the British were to be successful.

The Indians did not arrive at Albany until the latter part of June, 1754.[58] The Mohawks, who lived only forty miles away, were the last to attend.[59] This caused various speculations. Some thought fear of the French kept them away. Detractors of William Johnson, who attended the conference, stated that he prevented the Iroquois Nations from being punctual.[60]

> Not a few thought it an artifice of Mr. Johnson's, who expected to rise into importance, from the reputation of a mighty influence over the Indians, kept them from punctual attendance; being very confident of a public request of the commissioners to go up and hasten their progress.[61]

The Congress convened on June 18, 1754. William Johnson and the Iroquois were pleased with the numerous presents given to the Indians by the various colonial governments. These amounted to great value and were appreciated.[62]

The Indians stated that in the previous colonial conflict,

King George's War, the British had abandoned Fort Saratoga and left the region unfortified. This fort was burned by order of Governor Clinton and abandoned because troops were needed for the expedition on Canada in 1746-1748.[63] In contrast, the French fortified and maintained their garrisons and thus protected their Indian allies.[64]

William Johnson spoke at the Congress and presented suggestions for defeating the French.[65] These included agreement with the Iroquois Nations that the British should fortify the Indian regions and negotiate with the Native Americans whenever possible.[66] He also helped settle a dispute between Connecticut and Pennsylvania.

Pennsylvanians had acted openly in negotiations for Iroquois land. At the same time, slippery Connecticut representative John Henry Lydius, secretly collected signatures for the same land. [67] Johnson intervened by later calling sachem Henrick to Mount Johnson to undo the mistake. Hendrick disapproved of what had transpired:

> as well as the weakness of those of his Brethren
> who were seduced by Lydius, and promised to do
> all he could to make them revoke or retract what
> they had so shamefully done.[68]

After this meeting with Henrick, the sachem journeyed to the nations of the confederacy to refute the Connecticut claim by Lydius. William Johnson also met with the Six Nations to resolve the situation. He persuaded the Iroquois to support the Pennsylvania claim which he believed was fair. It was obvious that his ability at persuasion and negotiation with the Indians was again at a very high level.

The conclusion of the Albany Congress, was that the British colonies united to a larger extent against the French. A common fund was created to defray all the military costs that would occur.[69] Also, it was suggested that the Iroquois territory would be fortified to protect the Six Nations against the French. In turn, the Indians agreed to furnish at least 1,000 braves to be used for general service.[70] Six hundred more were to be raised to help repel any attack on Oswego by the French. The leader of the Indians would be William Johnson.[71] Thus, his leadership was evident during the Albany Congress as it had been in the past.

By the year 1754, the last colonial war between France and Britain commenced. The British claimed French expansion in the Ohio Valley as a main reason. The French king stated that it was

> England, in the year 1754 that was the aggressor in the contests concerning the settlement in North America; and that in the month of June the British fleet, in contempt of the laws of nations and the faith of treaties began to commence the most violent hostilities against the ships of his majesty and the navigation and commerce of his subjects.[72]

William Johnson experienced the aggression of the French by 1754 in his own region and began to organize militarily for the war. In his orders of June 6th to the officers of the Second Battalion, Johnson stated

> Whereas I have received severall Accounts of the French of <Canada> threatning a Discent on some part of this County, and last Night an Express arrived at my House importing the same, and that they were Actually Marched. Wherefore I think it for His Majesty's Service, as well as the safety of the Inhabitants of this County in particular that the Militia be kept in such Order, and readiness as that they may be fitt to March at a Moments Notice should the French attempt any such thing as from their Proceedings lately, and daily Behaviour we have no reason to doubt they may.[73]

In 1755, William Johnson again began to persuade Native Americans to fight with the British. On February 7th, he had a meeting with the Mohawks and Canajoharies.[74] Only seventeen days later, he was nominated by Governor William

Shirley as commander of the Crown Point expedition.[75] The Governor's reason for choosing the New York landlord were revealed in a letter he wrote to James DeLancey. The letter stated:

> The Gentleman I have thought of on this important Occasion is Collonel William Johnson of Mount Johnson in the Mohawk Country whose distinguished Character for the great Influence He hath for Severall Years Maintained over the Indians of the Six Nations is the circumstance, who, determines me in my choice preferably to any Gentleman in my own Governt tho there are not wanting there Officers of Rank, and Experience, out of Whom I could have Nominated one.[76]

In April, 1755, William Johnson set out for Alexandria, Virginia. On April 14, he was made superintendent of Indian affairs and commander of the Crown Point expedition.[77] On April 16th, he was commissioned major general by Governors Shirley and DeLancey.[78] A major reason why he obtained this high rank was that both governors felt his influence over Native Americans in general could be a deciding factor in the outcome of the war.

As spokesman for the Indians and a major general of the British Crown, Johnson did his best to secure fair treatment for all Native Americans. For instance, he persuaded Governor Shirley of Massachusetts to pay the Indians as a way to keep them loyal to the British. A letter from Shirley to Johnson on May 24, 1755 reveals this.[79] It states;

> I am intirely of your Opinion with regard to the Indian Officers, and will lose no time in pressing the several Governmts concern'd forthwith to make the needfull Provision for their Pay in the manner propos'd by you; as also for defraying the Expense of engaging and maintaining the Indians in the English Interest by fix'd Funds, and giving you an absolute Power to draw upon them for that Service accord-

ing to their respective proportions; which is doubt-
less necessary to be done.[80]

Besides providing salaries and equipment for the Iroquois,
the New York General organized "the Indians into Companys of
100 men each."[81] Those who were deemed interpreters among
the Indians, took "care of them in all respects, besides doing
their Duty as officers."[82] Johnson, in every way, tried to be fair
to the Indians and especially to his Mohawk neighbors in order
to keep them away from French influence and on the side of the
British. In a letter to Governor Shirley, he clearly stated his
opinion of the value the great expense of Indian influence
would bring. He stated;

> If we should Chastize the Insolence of the French,
> drive them from their Encroachments and maintain
> our conquests, I dare prophecize with common pru-
> dence on our side, the French will not rule a Nation
> of Indians on the Continent, and the Inhabitants of
> these Colonies will reap a thousand fold for their
> present Expenses and enjoy their possessions in
> uninterrupted security.[83]

The expenditures the English spent on the Iroquois had
long range influence on other Indians. Western Indian nations,
because of the great influence of the Six Nations, again used
the members of the Confederation as middlemen for the
English fur trade. The Indians of the mid-west indirectly
became English allies. William Johnson's gifts and fair practices not only attracted the Iroquois Nations, but many other
Indian nations away from the French.

Johnson's gifts to the Indians were varied. At times they
consisted of food and drink for large scale parties. He once
suplied an ox and many gallons of rum and a barrel of beer.[84]

> There were acts of piety: 'six gallons rum to bury
> two women who died in the Mohawk's castle in one
> night.' Charity was always needed, either wholesale
> — he clothed entire tribes — or retail — 'a blan-
> ket, shirt, stockings, kettle, salt, and cash to a poor

widow, a mother of a young man who was killed in Canada by the French.' Leading Indians were propitiated in groups — he had hats trimmed with lace a hundred at a time and bought dozens of red boxes to hold crowns — or singly: 'To Hendrick's son, a banyan. . .some silver work as breast buckles, etc.' Guns, axes and knives were mended; ribbons supplied to brighten braves' hair; and horses lent to help squaws with their plowing. Seed 'for sweeter corn than they ever had' made furrows speak with an English tongue, and the inoculations of papooses against smallpox — fifty-four, for instance, at one time.[85]

From 1755 until the end of the French and Indian War in 1763, Johnson had numerous conferences with the Six Nations and other Indians. He was able to persuade the Indians to side with the British or at least stay neutral through the use of dialogue.[86] His rhetorical ability was considerable, and he used it often.

Many of the conferences with the Indians were held at Fort Johnson. Some were held at the Indian castles. Johnson had meetings with Native Americans wherever he thought they would do the most good. A large number of these influenced the Native Americans during the ongoing war.

On December 7, 1755, William Johnson held a conference at Fort Johnson with the Mohawks, Oneidas, Tuscaroras and Senecas.[87] He stated that the Shawnees, Delaware and River Indians were committing hostilities against the British. He stated that they burned settlements and killed "people who had never offended them."[88] He asked the Iroquois to ... "without loss of time reprimand them for what they have already done, prevent them from doing any more mischief."[89] He also stated that he wanted the Six Nations to insist that these Indians turn:

> their arms with us against the French and their Indians; both your and our common enemy and with out loss of time. This is what you engaged to

do at the general meeting last June at my house: I am surprised you have not done it before and I expect you will not do it without loss of time; if not you will endeavour to put a stop to their barbarities, and do ourselves that justice the laws of nature allows.[90]

At the meeting cited, Johnson also asked the Iroquois to send him any information that their allies revealed to them. In turn, he promised to pass on any information that he felt was important to the said Indians.[91]

William Johnson was made a baronet only a few days before the conference in question on November 27, 1755.[92] Thus, for the remainder of this study, he will be referred to as Sir William. The reason for the title will be described later on.

The Mohawks, Senecas, Oneidas and Tuscaroras replied to Sir William that they were greatly concerned about the hostilities that he mentioned. They assured him that they would forward his message to all nations concerned.[93] The Indians stated further that they would:

use all arguments in their power for the exerting themselves on this important occasion. We will also recommend it to them to keep up a constant correspondence with you, as we are sensible it is of the utmost consequence at all times but more so at the present.[94]

On December 26, 1755, Sir William had another meeting with the Mohawks, Oneidas and Tuscaroras.[95] Sequareesere, a chief of the Tuscaroras, spoke for the Indians. He thanked Johnson for supplying them with ammunition, large guns and paint.[96] He stated further that:

as we do not know how soon the enemy will come upon us: we have been speaking to our eldest brothers these four years, about having a place of defence made against the French, but could never bring them to a conclusion until now, having promised to Join and assist our brothers the

66

English against any attempts which the French shall make upon them.[97]

The conference continued with discussions of the French encroaching upon the hunting grounds of the Indians.[98] The Iroquois suggested that a British fort be built immediately in their territory.[99] They also wanted "men to garrison it as we are certain the French only wait a favourable opportunity to fall upon us."[100] Sir William, in turn, promised to do what he could to have the fort built.

Throughout the French and Indian War, Johnson met with the Six Nations and other Indians numerous times to persuade them to stay away from the French. Time and time again he referred to the French as the enemies of the Indians. Also, in almost every case, he promised to give the Native Americans assistance in their plight. On February 2, 1756, he stated to the Oneidas, Tuscaroras, Skanidaradighronos, Chugnuts and Mahickanders, that they were far:

> from being safe, having so dangerous and decietful an enemy, as the French are notoriously known to be on one side, and their blind, folded, rash Indians (who know not their own interest) on the other. Wherefore, agreeable to your request, I shall immediately have a fort built for the safety of your old people, children and friends, living round about there; I will also supply you with arms, ammunition, etc. to defend the said fort against any attempts the French or their Indians, may make upon you. [101]

Johnson ended this speech by stating that if they needed him, he would come immediately to their assistance.[102]

The answer to the February 2, 1756 speech of Sir William was given by the Aughquageys, Tuscaroras, Skania-dara-dighronos, Mahickanders, Chugnuts and Shawanese. Adam, who was speaker for the Indians, stated that "this critical time lays us under the greatest obligations and be assured we and ours shall never forget it as long as the waters of Susquehanna run."[103]

At a private meeting on February 18, 1756, Sir William met with the Mohawks. A number of sachems and warriors were present. Abraham, Hendrick's brother, stood up and spoke for the Indians.[104] Abraham thanked Johnson for fortifying their castle and asked him to garrison it for the protection of their old people and children. Abraham stated that daily they had received reports "of the French intention of attacking us for our attachment to you."[105] Johnson answered his Mohawk brothers with the following statement:

> As I am fully convinced of your sincerity and attachment to his Majesty's interest, I readily comply with your request, not doubting it will be very agreeable to your Father the king, who has nothing more at heart than the safety and welfare of you his faithful children; as an assurance of what I say, and now promise to you I give you this belt of Wampum.[106]

It is quite obvious that Sir William did all he could to defend the Iroquois Nations and other Indians. In turn, he persuaded them to side with the British during the ongoing war. He did this with full knowledge that his kindness and promises of protection for the Native Americans were primarily for the British cause. Although Sir William truly respected the Indians, he showed time and time again that he was first and foremost an official of the British Crown.

At a meeting of five hundred and eighty six of the Six Nations and their allies in February of 1756, Sir William Johnson addressed the Seneca Indians. They were the most remote member of the Iroquois Confederation and the one most influenced by the French. Therefore, Sir William felt that keeping the Senecas neutral was mandatory.

The Senecas had had a minor skirmish with the British shortly before Johnson met with them. The meeting took place shortly after Sir William had become Sole Agent and Superintendent of the Indians and their Affairs.[107] Johnson obviously wasted no time in doing his job by meeting with the

Senecas on February 18, 1756, one day after his appointment.[108]

Sir William faced the Senecas with the same vigor that he revealed in all his conferences with Native Americans. His words indicate that the art of diplomacy was Sir William's strength. Johnson stated:

> I have heard with great concern that a war party of the Senecas the most remote nation of the confederacy, have had a considerable misunderstanding with their brethern the English to southward, which had been fatal to some of that nation. I am extremely unable to express my concern for that unhappy affair; and as the hatchet remains fixed in your heads, I do with the greatest affection and tenderness remove it thence.
>
> I am informed that upon that unhappy occassion you have left three of your principal warriors; I do with this belt cover their dead bodies offend our fight any more, and bury the whole affair in eternal oblivion.[109]

The Six Nations of Iroquois, including the Senecas, answered Sir William with thanks for his concern and great affection.[110] They acknowledged the harmony that the confederation had always had with the British.[111] They promised to pay due attention to his advice, which tended to be in the interest of their welfare and assured him that the unfortunate affair would be buried in oblivion.[112]

On February 24, 1756, the Senecas elaborated on what was said earlier at Fort Johnson. At this time, they recognized Sir William Johnson's ability to supply them with the necessities of life "cheaper and better than the French could possibly do."[113] They stated that such treatment would greatly tend to cement that friendship that subsists between us."[114] Obviously, Johnson had influenced them to a great extent and steered them away from a French alliance much more than would have been thought possible. He also helped resolve an unfortunate incident in which the Senecas had lost three war-riors.[115] To turn such a situation into a positive relationship between the Senecas and the British was a tremendous feat indeed. The incident reveals the value of Sir William Johnson's ability to negotiate with the Indians. In this instance, as in so many others, the Senecas revealed their great love and respect for the famed New Yorker. They stated:

> Brother Warraghijagey We are sensible of your goodness expressed to us in removing the cause of our grief and tenderly taking the ax out of our heads. We are thankful to you for cleaning the blood out of our fight agreeable to the ancient customs of our forefathers.[116]

Throughout February of 1756, Johnson met with numerous Indians for the British cause. In all cases, he repeated why the Native Americans should not side with the French. In all cases, he offered to supply and protect them. For instance, on February 27, Sir William promised the Oghquagoe Indians that he would build a trading house for them.[117] On the same day, he promised the Onondagas that he would build a fort for the protection of their castle. [118]

During the French and Indian War, Sir William Johnson had conferences with Native American groups over forty-five times.[119] He lectured them many times on what he wanted them to do. His rhetoric revealed his kindliness, but also the discipline he expected.

Johnson probably had more influence with the Mohawks than with any other tribe of the Confederation or with any other Indians. Possibly the simplest reason for this was that Johnson had settled in eastern New York which was the terri-tory of the Mohawks. Obviously, he would have a better chance to know this tribe than those tribes who resided far-ther away from his home. This was possibly the reason why the Senecas, the farthest tribe away from Mount Johnson, sup-ported the French more than did the other tribes of the confederation. In spite of this situation, Sir William spent many hours trying to persuade them.[120]

The Mohawks' respect for the man they called Warraghiyagey can be revealed by the great tract of land they offered to give him in 1761.[121] Supposedly almost every member of the tribe signed the deed that was given to him. Many colonials have stated that Johnson instigated this action and that the Indians had no right to give him such presents. Cadwallader Colden wrote the Board of trade stating that Johnson had circumvented regulations under the pretense of a gift.[122] However, the primary sources do not reveal this to be factual. Possibly those who spread such stories were jealous of Sir William. Naturally, the Mohawks would rather give their land to an old and trusted friend, who spoke their language and respected their culture, rather than eventually surrender it to strangers.

Another reason for Sir William's influence over the Mohawks was that he cohabited with Mohawk women[123] and was not ashamed to admit it. It was common practice for white traders, merchants, etc., to have sexual relations with Native American women. It was not common practice to do it openly rather than in secret. It is well known that Johnson was a man who could not live without women and that his sexual philosophy was extremely liberal for his time. However, his openness about his relations won him tremendous respect among Native American leaders.

The accepted version of William Johnson's spouses included Catherine Weissenberg; Mary Brant, mentioned in the first section of this project; and Caroline Peters, niece of his friend Sachem Hendrick.[124] Augustus Buell discusses Caroline in his biography of Sir William Johnson.[125] However, Milton Hamilton stated that there is no evidence that she ever existed.[126] In any case, cohabiting with Mohawk women and having parties with large groups of Indians made Johnson one of them in every way. A man with his high level of social acceptance would be very influential during the on-going war.

Johnson lived with, befriended, and cohabited with the Mohawks. They, in turn, sided with their white brother when hostilities arose.

During the war years, Sir William spoke often to Indians that were not part of the great Confederacy. He realized that indirectly any tribe that did not at least remain neutral in the war hurt the British cause. He, therefore, began to make treaties, not only with the Iroquois Nations but with such Nations as the Shawnees and Nanticokee, who lived on the western branch of the Susquehanna. The proceedings and treaty with the Indians just mentioned, was negotiated at Fort Johnson from April 14 to April 23, 1757. At this conference, Johnson described in his biased opinion the differences between the English and the French. He stated;

> I will tell you the difference between the English and the French. The English desire and labour to unite all Indians into one general Bond of brotherly love, and National Interest. The French endeavour to divide the Indians and stir up War and Contention amongst them. Those who intend to destroy or enslave any People or Nation will endeavor to divide them. — This you and all the Indians upon the Continent, Know has always been, and continues to be, the Endeavours of the French.
>
> Not less unaccountable is it Brethren, that the French should be able to persuade the Indians, that building Forts in the Middle of their Country and Hunting Grounds, is for their Interest and Protection. I tell you brethren, and warn you, that whatever good Words the French may give you — how much soever they may now smile on you — whatever presents they may now make you, your chains are in their pockets, and when their Designs are ripe for Execution, they will take the Axe out of their Bosom and strike it into your heads.[127]

The response to Johnson's speech was given on April 21st. The speaker thanked Sir William for his warm reception and concern for the long journey that the Indians had undertaken to reach Fort Johnson.[128] They assured him "that when their people at Home, shall hear of their entering into this agreement of Peace and Friendship, they will, we are sure, be exceedingly rejoiced."[129] They also stated that they would not only faithfully observe the treaty, but that they would teach it to their children.[130]

Concerning the French, the response of the Indians to Sir William's words were as follows;

> All you said to us concerning the Difference of Conduct between the English and the French, and everything you desired us to publish among our People, and all the Nations, gave us great Satisfaction; and we think it to be the Truth.[131]

Johnson stressed to the Indians that after the treaty was made, he desired the Shawnees and Nanticokes to pass on any information that they heard that would help the British cause. Sir William realized that although these Indians were not in his geographical region, they could be of real value by relaying information concerning French plans or movements about the war. The Indians responded by going along with his wishes. They stated:

> You have desired, that whenever we hear anything which may concern the interest or welfare of our Brethren the English, we should without Delay communicate it. You may depend that we will do this; and if we get any intelligence, through the Middle of the Night, we will send off an Express to you. Some of our young People are generally on the Hunt, and are very likely to make discoveries.[132]

From 1755 until the war ended, Sir William Johnson applied his rhetorical skills in order to get the Iroquois tribes to fight with the British. The Mohawks indirectly had already agreed to fight. The rest of the Confederation and the other Indians were not as willing to go against the French. Johnson appealed to each important Indian with arguments, presents and long range promises. He was generally very fatigued after long hours of persuasion. However, even when he thought he had only been moderately successful, or less, he did not give up. His will was made of iron, and his ability to convince others was his strong point. During the first few years of the war, his influence over the Indians was substantial. In fact, large numbers of natives outwardly supported his cause. This is evident from a letter he wrote to Lieutenant Colonel Ellison on June 30, 1755.[133] The letter states in part:

> I am surrounded by upwards of 1000 Indians, <Men> Women and Children, and tho I am extreamly impatient <to> be at Albany in order to look after and forward <the affairs of place until I have finished those Affairs with the Indians which at present require my uninterrupted Attention. I hope in a few days to settle Matters wth them as to be able to leave this place.
> Yesterday the Indians of the 9 Nations here present declared they would join and Assist their Bretheren the English in our present undertakings against the french.[134]

As the French and Indian War ravaged on, it became painfully obvious that keeping the Indians loyal to Britain, or at least neutral, was no easy task. However, in 1755, only a year after the war began, Sir William seemed very successful.[135] A letter to James DeLancey on July 10th of that year reveals the influence that Johnson felt he had had up to that point with the Iroquois.[136] He stated;

> Last Saturday my Conferences with the Indians ended. I have only time at Present to Advise you that they made an unanimous Declaration that they would stand by their Bretheren the English and would in no shape assist the French. In this I have abundant reason to believe them sincere and that the whole Confederacy are at present more warmly disposed toward our Interest than they have been for these 40 years past.[137]

CHAPTER 5

The Iroquois and Other Indians as Valuable Allies

Wwilliam Johnson's influence on the Iroquois Nations and other Indians was a valuable aid to the British in the last two colonial wars. During King William's War, his influence was marginal because very little of the European-based conflict occurred in North America. However, in the last colonial conflict between France and Britain, Johnson's influence was much greater, and the Native Americans were a major strategic factor. This has been alluded to by many historians, but not definitely affirmed by any until now.

The French and Indian War began over the expansion and control of the Ohio Valley.[1] Early in 1755, Major General Edward Braddock was sent to America to free the Ohio from French control.

> Braddock's orders were nevertheless positive - For the preservation of Oswego and the reduction of Niagara, it was at length agreed, that Shirley's and Pepperel's regiments should proceed to Lake Ontario - while General Braddock attacked Fort Duquesne - and the provincial troops, commanded by General Johnson marched to invest Crown Point.[2]

Braddock landed in Virginia with a body of troops to

accomplish his mission. His march toward Fort Duquesne and eventual defeat on the Monongahela, are well recorded.[3] On July 9th, 1755, about eight miles from the fort, a force of French and Indians attacked the British. Indian accounts stated that Braddock's 2,200 troops were routed by only 400 of the enemy.[4] The celebrated Battle of the Wilderness ended with a British retreat after three hours of confusion.[5] General Braddock was mortally wounded and died shortly thereafter.

It was known that Edward Braddock did not like provincials and had little respect for Indians.[6] "Nevertheless, he took some pains to secure their aid, and complained that Indian affairs had been so ill-conducted by the provinces that it was hard to gain their confidence. "[7] This was obviously the reason why, less than three months before his death, he commissioned Sir William Johnson as sole manager of the Six Nations and their allies.[8] The letter stated;

> Alexandria, 15th April 1755
> By His Excellency Edward Braddock Esqr General & Commander in Chief of all His Majestys Forces in North America
>
> To William Johnson Esqr.
> By Virtue of the Power and Authority to me given and granted by His Majesty to appoint a proper Person or Persons to have the sole management and direction of the Affairs of the Six Nations of Indians and their Allies, to the end that the said Indians may be heartily engaged in and attached to the British Interest, I do hereby appoint you the said William Johnson in the Name and behalf of His Majesty to superintend and manage the Affairs of the said Nations and their Allies, giving you full Power and Authority to treat and confer with them as often and upon such matters as you shall judge necessary for His Majestys Service.[9]

After Braddock's death, William Shirley of Massachusetts

was put in charge of British forces in North America. Shirley decided to build an English fort near Crown Point on Lake George to check the French advance from Canada. To act general of this expedition, he picked Sir William Johnson of New York. Johnson was to build the aforementioned fort, and then proceed to attack Crown Point.

A rift had developed between Governor Shirley and Sir William before Braddock's death. Shirley had questioned the authority Johnson had received from Braddock and Johnson's right to requisition supplies.[10] There was also a disagreement over funds to supply the Indians that would accompany Johnson to Crown Point. Finally, Shirley honored the New Yorker's request concerning the Native Americans, although the problems between the two men was far from resolution.[11]

The problems between Shirley and Johnson were further complicated by Shirley's need to have Indians join his march to Niagara. Johnson did not want to order this, for the Indians Shirley wanted were to be part of his force marching to Crown Point. Also, Johnson insisted that Shirley did not need any Indians until he reached Oswego. However, to appease Shirley, he did ask three tribes to provide the governor with help.[12]

The matter between Johnson would have ended if Shirley had not begun to question the New York leader at every turn. Shirley even employed John Henry Lydius and others to attain Indians for his Niagara campaign.[13] This convinced Johnson that Governor "Shirley meant to wreck his Indian influence."[14] It seemed to Sir William that the slippery Lydius would not only hurt his interests, but the British cause as well.

Sir William Johnson proceeded to the Carrying Place on August 9th, 1755.[15] On August 18th, he began one of two forts that would be built in the area.[16] He arrived at Lake Saint Sacrement on August 28th, and renamed it Lake George on September 1st, 1755.[17] He was obviously not insubordinate to his superior, but yet vented his anger in a letter to Thomas Pownall on September 4, 1755, only four days before the battle of Lake George.[18] The letter stated in part:

I have lately received a long <letter from General>

Shirley tis in Answer to one I wrote him and if I <had time> to send you the Copy of it, you would only be con<fused un>less I would also send you a former I recd from him <and my> answer wch are at Albany. This Letter is wrote with all <the> Insolence of a Man drunk with power, envenomed by Malice and burning with Revenge - his Arguments are weak and confused they bear the evident Marks of Passion overruling Reason - he asser<ts> Facts notoriously false, and attempts to very clumsily, artfully to per-vert all my Actions and Arguments.[19]

After the Battle of Lake George, Johnson, still upset with Governor Shirley, offered his resignation to his commander in chief on November 9th.[20] Shirley declined the resignation, partly because of his need for Johnson's services, and partly because of what had happened at the battle.

The Battle of Lake George was a major chapter in Sir William Johnson's life. Before this time, he had not fought in any battle or any previous engagement. It must be remem-bered that in King George's War, although he had organized the Indians into a fighting force, he, himself, had not taken part. His lack of experience was noted not only by many of his critics, but by himself. Yet, he ventured with determination and courage into his first military engagement.

Johnson pitched his camp at the south side of the Lake.[21] He immediately sent out scouts to spy on the French.[22] He wrote to James DeLancey shortly after his arrival;

I arrived here with about 1500 men the 28<th> past in the Evening, all was thick Wood, not a Foot of Land cleared, Our time since has been chiefly spent in opening the Ground about us and forming some regular kind of Encampment building temporary Store houses for Provisions and these Matters are now nearly accomplished. We have fixt on a Spot for the Fort it is clearing and near 400 Men employed, who I hope in a few days will have the Fort in great forwardness and that it will be put into a respectable Condition before the Army leaves this place.[23]

Early in the year of 1755, the French sent a force of 3,000 troops to Quebec. They were commanded by Baron Dieskau, a veteran of many campaigns in Europe.[24]

Dieskau planned to attack Oswego, but changed his mind because he believed William Johnson's "thrust toward Crown Point was the more immediate danger."[25]

Dieskau learned that Johnson was marching from Fort Edward to Lake St. Sacrement, or Lake George. He decided to attack Fort Edward with a small force of "1,400 men (600 Canadians, 600 Indians, and 200 French grenadiers)."[26] However, the French Indians decided they did not want to face the guns of the fort and "preferred to attack William Johnson's open camp."[27]

Johnson's scouts reported to him that the French were threatening Fort Edward. Johnson, in a Council of War, decided to send 1,000 men and Indians to relieve the fort.[28] However, they were ambushed by the French and Colonel Ephraim Williams and a number of other British officers were killed. As Johnson stated in this engagement, we suffered our greatest loss.[29]

> Colonel Williams, major Ashley; captain Farrell, brother-in-law to the general, who commanded a party of Indians, captain Stoddart, captain McGinnes, captain Stevens, all Indian officers, and the Indians say near forty of their people, who fought like lions, were all slain.[30]

Old Hendrick, the great Mohawk chief, was also killed during the ambush.[31] Sir William was extremely sad over this loss, for Hendrick had been a close friend for many years. The only comforting thought was that his old friend died fighting fiercely against the French. Among the enemy dead was Mons. St. Pierre who had commanded the French Indians.[32]

The remainder of the British force retreated to Lake George. Johnson barely had time to throw up barricades when the enemy appeared in sight at approximately eleven thirty.[33] The French marched directly toward the center of the British force:

> They made a small halt about 150 yards from our Breast-Work, when the regular Troops (whom we judged to be such by their bright and fixed Bayonets) made the grand center Attack) the Canadians and Indians squatted and dispersed on our Flanks - The Enemy's Fire we received first from their Regulars in Platoons, but it did no great Execution, being at too great Distance, an our Men defended by the Breast-Work - Our Artillery then began to plan on them, and was served under the Direction of captain Eyre during the whole Engagement in a manner very advantageous to his Character. The engagement now became general on both sides.[34]

The battle raged for five hours.[35] "The French tried a flank attack on Johnson's right, which was repulsed by the Massachusetts regiments of Titcomb and Ruggles."[36] At about four o'clock, the British jumped over the Breast-Work and pursued the French.[37] The British Indians slaughtered the enemy in great numbers and took Baron Dieskau prisoner.[38] Dieskau had been badly wounded in the leg and through both his hips.[39] The wounds were so severe that the surgeon feared for his life.[40]

Ludwig August von Dieskau was a German baron in the service of France.[41] He realized that in order to be victorious over Johnson's superior force, he would have to depend on a surprise attack and did not want the British troops to attack the smaller French group.[42] As it turned out, Johnson's raw militiamen were able to overcome the French. Johnson's force of 3,500 colonials, mostly New Englanders and 400 Indians, far outnumbered the French. It would have been extremely difficult for the French to win the battle. As already stated, Dieskau had only 1,400 men at Lake George, although Johnson stated the French force was possibly as large as 2,300.[43] Sir William exaggerated the enemy numbers so as to make his victory seem more impressive.

During the early part of the battle, Johnson received a rifle ball in his thigh.[44] His secretary, Peter Wraxall, saw the incident and thought it a mortal wound.[45] Luckily, the wound, although painful, was not serious. Johnson played down the wound, and although it was dressed, the ball was not removed.[46] He directed the battle as best he could, although he was removed to his tent when his leg stiffened.

The victory at Lake George belonged to William Johnson. He was the British commander, and received the credit for winning the battle.[47] However, although his fame and stature grew after Lake George, historians such as Francis Parkman do not believe it was well deserved. Parkman believed that Phineas Lyman deserved credit for the victory because he took over command of the British forces when Johnson retired to his tent.[48] This view does have some merit, in fact, for Lyman was in the heat of battle for over four hours and Johnson was wounded shortly after the battle began. Parkman's criticism of Johnson can be detected from the following passages:

> He himself (Johnson) found no lack of eulogists; and to quote the words of an able but somewhat caustic and prejudiced opponent, 'to the panegyrical pen of his secretary Mr. Wraxall, and the sic volo sic jubeo of Lieutenant-Governor DeLancey, is to be ascribed that mighty renown which echoed through the colonies, reverberated to Europe, and elevated a raw inexperienced youth into a kind of second Marlborough.' Parliament gave him five thousand pounds, and made him a baronet.[49]

Johnson's force did not follow up their victory at Lake George because they anticipated another attack by a larger French force. Peter Wraxall discussed this strategy in a letter to Henry Fox on September 27, 1755, nineteen days after the battle[50] Wraxall stated that, "The Enemy's Forces ready to oppose Us are more than We should with the expected Reinforcements be able to march against them.[51]

Francis Parkman strongly believed that Johnson should have pursued the French after lake George and that his caution was a major blunder.[52] However, throughout his writing, Parkman reveals disdain for Sir William and his criticism has to be kept in perspective when searching for the truth.

Milton Hamilton arrived at a much more favorable evaluation, arguing that the Indians had departed and could not be persuaded to return, and that terms of enlistments were running out and many soldiers wanted to return to their farms.[53] Earlier writers such as Augustus Buell stated that

> after deducting the losses in the battle of Lake George, and taking account of the fact that most of the Indians returned to their homes soon afterward, thus reducing Johnson's force to less than 2,400 all told, it appears reasonable that he should pause at the idea of attempting to storm or even besiege a regular fortification like Crown Point.[54]

During the Lake George battle the losses to the British were over 156 men,, according to Seth Pomeroy, who fought in the battle.[55] This does not count the forty Iroquois who were killed or the number of British who were listed as missing. That the battle was costly, can be detected from a letter from Seth Pomeroy to his sister-in-law on September 11, 1755, three days after the battle.[56] Pomeroy stated;

> This brings heavy tidings. But let not your heart singue at the news tho it be your loss of a Dear Husband. Monday the 8 instant was a memorable day, and truly you may say had not the Lord been on our side we must all ben swallowed up. My brother being one that went out in the first engagement after fighting a considerable time, received a fatal shot through the middle of the head.[57]

The deciding factor at Lake George was not Sir William Johnson's influence on the Iroquois. His superior force simply overpowered the French. However, there is evidence that Johnson's influence over the Indians did help the outcome and the treatment of Baron Dieskau. Dieskau related that he owed Johnson his life for persuading the Iroquois to allow him to live after he was wounded and captured.

> As it had not been for Johnson he (Dieskau) should have assuredly burned at a slow fire by the Iroquois who wished to oblige to avenge the death of three of their chiefs killed in action.[58]

Over four hundred members of the Iroquois Nations fought bravely at Lake George.[59] These Native Americans definitely helped Sir William win the battle by their mere presence. If the four hundred Iroquois had not accompanied Sir William to Lake George and fought bravely, he would not have had the numerical advantage in numbers during the battle. Obviously, the British were directly helped by the Iroquois Nations at Lake George.

The British also were helped, indirectly during the battle by Sir William Johnson's influence over the Iroquois Nations and other Indians. This was the case, even though he had some trouble controlling the Indians who fought on the British side. Johnson's indirect influence had to do with the French Indians who fought against Sir William's forces.

The French Indians did not want to kill the Iroquois members, and thus helped the British win. For instance, during the ambush of Colonel Williams, the French Indians stood and shot straight in the air to warn their fellow Iroquois of the French ambush.[60] Baron Dieskau ordered the French and Indians to attack the British.[61] The attack took place shortly, "except the Iroquois, who did not budge."[62]

The French pursued the British force closely, but the Indians, especially the Iroquois, were at a distance.[63] The Iroquois under Johnson thus influenced the outcome of the French ambush and allowed much of the British force to escape back to Lake George. By persuading four hundred Indians to accompany him to Lake George, he had indirectly influenced the outcome of an early part of the battle that favored the British. If the French Indians had not warned their fellow Iroquois or pursued them vigorously, most likely all of the 1,000 member advance force would have been killed. In actuality, many escaped and returned to Johnson's main force.

As the French headed for Lake George after the ambush, the French Indians again gave the British the advantage. The French had to halt before attacking the British force because of disputes among the Indians.[64] Most likely the French did not want to undertake a frontal attack on a superior force when they saw Johnson's artillery.

The French Indians, including the Cagnawagas, considered the bravest of the lot,[65] did not want to make a frontal attack on Johnson's cannon. They veered off to the sides of the British force and gave Johnson's army time to tighten their defenses.[66] These fifteen minutes were crucial and contributed to the French defeat.[67]

Baron Dieskau had trouble with his Indians on two separate occasions, and, thus, lost the battle. Johnson's Indians indirectly cut short the ambush of Colonel William and fought bravely. Many Native Americans were killed or wounded during both engagements. They were not the major reason why the British won at Lake George, but definitely helped in the victory.

Assessing the Battle of Lake George logically, it seems nearly impossible that Baron Dieskau could have overcome the much larger British force under Johnson.[68] Johnson's inexperience and Dieskau's tenacity and military genius almost made the French victorious. However, because of numbers, the odds were with the British and they won quite decisively.

William Johnson, who, because of his victory at Lake George, became Sir William Johnson, was bestowed praise and congratulations for defeating the French. His capture of General Baron Dieskau helped even the score for Braddock and hurt French prestige. [69] Friends such as Hubert Marshal marvelled at Johnson's great success.[70] Referring to the baronet given Johnson by the crown, Marshal stated;

> Am truly Glad of the Honour You have Obtained which I hope will Increase In Your Compleat Triumph over Our Enemys Pardon and More but hope this will find You in Perfect Health.[71]

Governors throughout the colonies expressed their gratitude and congratulation. Colonial cities had special celebrations. Newspapers wrote the story of the great victory. All the British colonies shared in Sir William's success. His fame and popularity soared and his friends urged him to seek public office.

In England, the name Sir William Johnson was discussed in the House of Commons.[72] Also, in his native country of Ireland, he received praise, thanks and ultimate fame. A letter dated January 31, 1756, reveals the pride which the Irish had for him.[73] It stated;

> Our whole kingdom is overjoy'd to find that this Success is owing to a gent of this countrey and say they could expect no less from the nephew of the Brave Sir Peter Warren and you can easily imagine what joy it has diffis'd among your own relatives and friends.[74]

After the battle of Lake George, Sir William's Indian influence, however, began to wane. The Indians threatened Johnson "with being abandoned by the whole nation."[75] To protect the French commander, Baron Dieskau, the New York general detached fifty men to guard him.

> Yet all these precautions did not prevent one of them entering his tent, sword in hand, on the morning following, to dispatch him; but an English officer, happening there by chance, threw himself before him, calling on the guard at the same time

for assistance; this obliged Chevalier de Johnson to have him removed to Orange.[76]

The Mohawks and other Indians who had fought with the British at Lake George soon left the battlefield to return home. They feared that the French Indians would retaliate on their families for siding with the English during the battle. Sir William's influence of the early war years changed after Lake George and diminished further in 1756-1758. Various incidents occurred in which the Indians were treated poorly. As a result, various Indians mutinied and turned on the British. Generally, by 1757, most of the Iroquois Nations were neutral. The Indians did not want to be on the losing side at the war's end. At this point in the confrontation, it was difficult to determine which side would be ultimately victorious.

On December 2, 1755, Sir William Johnson resigned command of the army he had led to victory at Lake George.[77] On January 3, 1756, Johnson declined Governor William Shirley's offer to accept a commission for Indian Affairs.[78] This gesture was because of the friction that occurred between Shirley and Johnson during the war. Shirley had sent Sir William a mass of absurd instructions on how to deal with the Indians. [79] Johnson replied that he was going to lay the whole affair before the king and ministry.[80] Finally, on February 17th, a royal commission was sent to Sir William, making him sole agent and superintendent of the Six Nations and other northern Indians.[81] This action settled his status for all time and stated once and for all that all matters concerning Indians must go through Sir William Johnson.[82]

As stated, Sir William's Indian influence was not as strong after Lake George. However, he would not be second to Shirley on this matter. In a letter to Governor Shirley from January 6, 1755, Johnson stated;

> As your Excellency has now determined that I shall act by General Braddocks Commission appointing me to the Sole Management of Indian Affairs, by which Commission All persons to whom the direction of the affairs of the Six Nations or their Allies

have been heretofore committed, and all other what-
soever are strictly required and enjoined to cease
and forbear acting or intermeddling therein.[83]

British influence on the Iroquois Nations and other Indians
continued to diminish considerably during the late 1750's.
There were several incidents between British troops and the
Indians which resulted in rifts between the two groups. The
Mohawks, who lived near Fort Johnson, let their horses loose
in Sir William's fields to do damage. They later apologized for
their actions and insisted they needed arms to fight the
French who were making their presence known in the
Mohawk valley. Johnson, at the time, was suffering from
pleurisy and violent stitches and had trouble turning in bed.
He tried to reassure the Mohawks that they would be protected by the Crown. Johnson even tried to stop them from leaving the valley by pretending he had legal authority to keep
them there.

The Iroquois Nations and other Indians had supported the
British during the early part of the French and Indian War.
This changed as the British began to lose ground to the
French. [84] The French, for instance, secured the assistance of
the Delaware and Shawnee Indians of the Pennsylvania area
and south.[85] These Native Americans ravaged the countryside and took English prisoners ... "in almost every one of
the Delaware Towns on the Susquehannah as high up as
Diahogo."[86]

Governor Robert Hunter Morris of Pennsylvania declared
war on the Delawares and the Shawnee Indians for attacking
the English.[87] He praised the work Sir William did with the
Indians, especially in colonies exposed greatly to the French
threat.[88] However, by his actions, he hurt the negotiations Sir
William was carrying on with the Six Nations, which concerned the behavior of these Indians. Johnson revealed this
information in a letter to Governor William Shirley, April 14,
1756.[89] The letter also indirectly discloses the trouble Johnson
had with the Iroquois Nations as a result of French influence
on Indians in general.[90] The letter states;

Sir Charles Hardy writes me that Governor Morris by the public prints had declared War against the Delawares and Shawanese Indians. I am surprized that Mr. Morris whose Province was so much interested in the result of the 6 Nations Embassy to those Indians, who was a principal in it and to whom I sent a Copy of my late Proceedings, would not wait to hear the effects of this Embassy he entered into this consequential Measure.

What will the Delawares and Shawanese think of such Opposition and contradiction in our Conduct? How shall I behave at the approaching meeting at Onondaga, not only to those Indians, but to the 6 Nations? These Hostile Measures wch. Mr. Morris has entered into, is throwing all our Schemes into Confusion, and must naturally give the 6 Nations such Impressions and the French such advantages to work on against us, that I tremble for the Consequences.[91]

Lord John Loudoun was made supreme commander of the British forces in North America in 1756. His delays and indecisions gave the French opportunities to win victories over the British. Loudoun further displayed his ineptitude by sailing off to attack the French fortress of Louisbourg.[92] He could not get within firing distance and had to return to New York City unsuccessful.

Since he left behind only enough troops to Garrison Fort Edward and William Henry, there was no hope that England's vanished prestige with the Indians would be restored that summer by any forest offensive or even an attempt to rebuild Oswego.[93]

In a fit of rage, Lord Loudoun made a further blunder. He felt it unimportant to keep the Six Nations as allies to the British, and pushed for all Indians who did not declare war on the French to be branded as enemies. Such an attitude was dangerous to the British and made Sir William's negotiations with the natives extremely difficult. This attitude went against the ideas of Johnson and also of Governor William Shirley, who favored protection of the Indians. He stated this in a letter to the Lords of Trade, on January 5, 1756.[94]

It was obvious to Johnson that many of the Iroquois during the late 1750's were not supporting the British, mainly because of British blunders and because the French were winning the war. The Senecas, for instance, were supporting the French by the late 1750's. If the Senecas were to be kept on the British side, or at least remain neutral during the last years of the war, Sir William would have to do extensive work.

The Iroquois Nations and other Indians wavered throughout the war, but yet indirectly helped Johnson and the British through an intelligence system designed to reveal French secrets. In this way, many times throughout the war, Sir William was able to get valuable information about the strength of the French, French movements, and about plans the French were to carry out against the British. For instance, on April 28, 1757, a Nanticoke Indian chief and a Connaye Indian arrived at Fort Johnson.[95] These Native Americans gave Johnson information about the French and their Indians.[96] The Nanticoke chief stated;

> At Fort duQuesne, he saw 400 Indians from the Westward and that at the next Fort to it were 300 more - that he saw the 400, Set off towards Potomack, which a number of French and 3 Officers - that the 300 were preparing to set off for Niagara, and were to go from thence to Oswego, where they were to be Joined by another Body from Canada; and that when these two Bodies met, they were to proceed downwards to the Mohawk River, and not stop until they came to Albany.[97]

The Indians who gave the news of French movements to Sir William were only a small part of the intelligence network that Johnson had set up. Through this system, Johnson's influence on the Iroquois Nations and other groups helped the British win the war. The Nanticoke chief, like so many other Native

Americans, had allegiance to Johnson and the British.[98] As he stated;

> Brother
> According to the Old Covenant between us, which ever party hears any News, that is of Consequence to the Other, they are to Communicate it, which we have now done, and shall Continue to do the same, as we are determined to stand by our Bretheren the English.[99]

During the late 1750's, Sir William Johnson was worried that the Six Nations were going to be completely alienated by the Crown. The best way to win the Indians' favor was by holding conferences and making treaties. Much of this was discussed in the preceeding chapter. In any case, the art of persuasion was very important at this time. On June 3, 1756, Sir William Johnson set out for one of the many conferences he attended. This one was at Onondaga.[100] On his way to Onondaga, Johnson also had conferences with Indians at Oneida.[101] He reached Onondaga on June 18, and conferred with the Iroquois until July 3, 1756.[102]

The Onondaga conference was important, for it won over many Native Americans who were favoring the French. The Six Nations and other Indians had become dissatisfied, "arising from the want of vigor which had so characterized the military operations of the English."[103]

> To such an extent had the disaffection spread, that it required a variety of arguments, and his utmost influence 'to expel the French poison and reanimate them to the English interest.' His efforts,, however, were so far successful, that the Six Nations expressed themselves as sincerely disposed to second any vigorous attempts that might be made against the French.[104]

The Iroquois also agreed to prevail upon their allies to unite and support the British.[105] They promised further to open up a road to Oswego and build a fort at Oswego Falls.[106] Johnson's status with the Native Americans at this point of the war was helping the conflict to end. The Iroquois Nations wanted the British to initiate a vigorous campaign against the French. Only then could they logically hurt the French and reveal to the Indians their military superiority.

The British generals who had command in 1756 and 1757 were incompetent, to say the least. Together, Lord Loudoun, General James Abercromby, and General Daniel Webb, almost lost the French and Indian War for Britain.[107] During this period, Sir William Johnson's Indian influence was at the lowest point in the war. The Iroquois Nations and other Indians had been influenced by Johnson throughout the early conflict, but leaned more and more toward the French during the later period because of British failures.

During the years in which Loudoun, Abercromby and Webb had command of British forces, Sir William Johnson's hands were tied. Loudoun brought the British cause

> to its most desperate state, to make French success almost universal from Lake Champlain to the Ohio, and to enshroud the hopeless colonies in a gloom that trenched closely upon the borders of despair.[108]

Abercromby was a brave soldier who just did not understand warfare in the wilderness of America. He felt he could do wonders by using the bayonet. His one effort was the assault on Fort Ticonderoga with 14,000 soldiers. The French general Moncalm defended the fort with only 3,600 troops. [109] The outcome was disastrous for the British who lost nearly 2,000 men in thirty minutes and then retreated in confusion.[110] Sir William, who led 500 Indians, mostly Mohawks, during this battle, was not permitted to do anything but share the disappointment of defeat.[111] The British had outnumbered the enemy by four to one. Francis Parkman believed that … "a gallant army was sacrificed by the blunders of its chief."[112]

General Webb shortly took over for Abercromby, but was possibly an even worse military leader. His sole exploit was to hold his army at Fort Edward while Moncalm besieged and took Fort William Henry only a few miles away.[113] His only advice to the British commander was of surrender.

It was obvious by 1758 that Sir William's influence over the Iroquois Nations and other Indians was almost non-existent. His best hope at the time was to keep the Indians neutral, and if possible, keep them from fighting with the French. He met with Indian groups over and over again to persuade them as best he could. He had over eight conferences with the Six Nations and other Indians in 1757 and 1758.[114] In late July, 1758, to hopefully get support for the British, he framed a peace treaty between the Iroquois Nations and southern Indians.[115] All of his fine diplomacy was only mildly successful at the time. The Six Nations, and even Sir William's beloved Mohawks were afraid to side with the British. It seemed to them by the astounding French victories, that the British would lose the war. A letter to Johnson from Thomas Butler and Jelles Fonda revealed how dangerous the Iroquois had become to the British by January, 1757.[116] The letter states;

> On hearing where Mr. Fonda was Going Said it was not Safe to Go among the Six Nations. And That he wou'd Stand a Chance To loose his Scalp among them.

> We came to the upper Castle of the Mohawks, went To the House of an Indian by the Name of Brant. Who Understanding We Were Going to the Six Nations told Some of our Company That if we Went Shou'd Certainly be killed or taken; That the upper Nations were not True in the English Intrist.[117]

The situation grew worse in that by 1757, the British Crown seriously considered hostilities against the Six Nations. Sir William realized that he could never convince the Iroquois Nations to remain neutral if the British made war on them. The situation was critical, for if the French continued winning the war, the Iroquois Nations would have definitely gone over to their side for good. Also, if the British treated the Iroquois Nations as enemies, they would lose Indian support forever.

Legend states that Sir William got seriously sick during the period and could not even turn in bed.[118] According to the story, Molly Brant, the Mohawk women, came to Johnson at this time and gave him the will to live.[119] Throughout the late 1750's, although Johnson was fatigued and tired at times, he continued to work to keep the Indians out of French control. There is no mention in the documents that he was close to death at this time, and was saved by Molly Brant.

During this period, when the odds were against him, when the French were winning the war, when his own Mohawk friends were deserting him, Sir William Johnson did his greatest service to the British Crown. He refused to give up and demonstrated the determination that has made him legendary. He met with the Indians again and again.

Fortunately for the British and for Johnson's cause, William Pitt came into power in 1757.[120] Pitt "became Secretary of State, with the lead of the House of Commons and full control of the war and foreign affairs." [121] Pitt committed the British government to unlimited warfare and, thus, the tide began to turn: "The hour had found the man."[122] Soon it was evident that the British would fight France to a standstill or, more likely, drive them out of North America for good.

The French, by 1758, were no longer the aggressor in the war. The presence of the Pitt regime was felt in less than a year. Also, the French had little to barter with the Indians by 1758.[123] Their own wheat crop had been a failure and few goods for the Indians were coming in from the mother country. This weakened the French influence over the Indians, for they had little to trade for pelts. Johnson suddenly found himself with an advantage over his enemy and a possible way to get the Six Nations and other Indians on the side of the British. He could outbid the French and buy Indian support. The door was now open for Johnson to recover his past prestige with the Iroquois Nations.

In the spring of 1758, Sir William again, with confidence,

took the role of the persuader and negotiator.[124] He also again began to send small war parties of Iroquois members into French territory as he did during King George's War. His position was strengthened as the British began to win victories in 1758 and 1759. Only a little over a year earlier in 1757, he could only muster approximately seventy Iroquois members to make treaties at Fort Johnson.[125] This all changed with British victories.

Also, after 1758, the British Navy was stopping ships from supplying the French Army.[126] Some of these supplies were used by Johnson to persuade the Iroquois Nations and other Indians to side with the British. Johnson "opened up a large store to them, where they, indeed, saw nothing but French goods."[127] As long as the goods held out, Sir William could regain some of his lost popularity.

Johnson realized that his message was again finding acceptance. The Mohawks were easy to persuade. Others, like the Onandagas, were another matter. Johnson set out to win these Indians over. He brought them provisions in territories still controlled by the French. When meeting Indians who were still on the French side, he bribed them with presents of brandy and other goods.[128]

As the British cause strengthened, William Pitt poured more troops, ammunition and supplies into America.[129] This made Sir William Johnson's job easier. He believed he could count on the Mohawks and other Iroquois Nations to fight the French. This was the case before William Pitt ordered James Abercromby to attack Ticonderoga. William Johnson accompanied Abercromby with 440 Indians.[130] Abercromby was defeated by Moncalm's much smaller force and routed. However, ultimately the defeat did not hurt Johnson's cause. General Abercromby ordered British troops to protect the Mohawk Valley and other Iroquois areas and to build Fort Stanwix. The Indians had never seen so many British troops before. This gave the natives a very strong reason to side with the British.[131]

As the Iroquois Nations and other Indians were again under

the influence of Sir William, the British benefitted three-fold. First, the Iroquois Nations did not fight with the French. Secondly, they sent warriors against the French. Thirdly, they influenced many other groups to desert the French and side with the British. As overloads they declared the Delawares at peace with the English and left French Fort Duquesne without allies.

As 1759 approached, the British had the advantage in the war. From July 22 to August 1, Johnson made a peace treaty between the Six Nations and southern Indians.[132] The western tribes also began to show support. Shortly thereafter, the Six Nations made it official that they would fight with the British. It was obvious at this time that the British would most likely win the war. The Iroquois Nations did not want to be on the wrong side.

During the spring of 1759, Sir William rallied a large force of Iroquois to march against Niagara. [133] In writing to the Board of Trade on May 17, 1759, he revealed a positive attitude concerning the support the Iroquois Nations would give the British.

> I think I may with great truth give it to your Lordship as my opinion, that not only from the commencement of the present War, but for many years past, His Majestys Indian Interests in this Quarter, hath not wore so favourable a Face nor given such encouraging Prospects. If the operations of His Majestys Arms in these parts, are carried don with Spirit and wear a respectable appearance on the opening of the Approaching campaign, I persuade myself the conduct of these Indians will be comfortable to the Promises they have made, and that they will convince the World by their actions they can be of very considerable Service to the Success of his Majestys Arms.
>
> If an attempt upon Niagara thro Lake Ontario should be part of the Plan of Operations for this

year, and that our Preparation for it, are projected with judgement and carried on with vigor, I am persuaded I could join His Majestys Troops that way, with the main Body of the Warriors of the Five Nations.[134]

The Battle of Niagara was fought in July of 1759.[135] Sir William led almost one thousand Iroquois Indians to Niagara.[136] They joined 2,200 colonial troops under the command of Brigadier General John Prideaux. Though two French vessels were cruising Lake Ontario and a large number of Indians were still under French control, no information regarding the British attack had reached Niagara. The French fort was greatly undermanned, for its troops had been sent to forts further south.

The British force landed on July 6th and, on the 20th, Prideaux was killed.[137] Immediately, Johnson vigorously assumed command. A letter to Frederick Haldimand of July 20, 1759, reveals this very well. The letter states in part;

> Sir/
> I am sorry to Inform You that this Evening We had the Misfortune to lose the General by one of our own Cohorts. As the Command devolves on me, I would have You imediately Join the Army here. If any Amunition can be spared from thence, I would have you order it here imediately, without waiting for it.[138]

The British realized that they could not take Niagara by assault and so laid siege. A large French force of twelve hundred troops and several Indians tried to reinforce Niagara, but were ambushed by a force sent out by Sir William. Johnson's Indian intelligence had informed him of the added manpower the French were going to receive and he dealt with this situation by pushing the French back whenever possible.

Command at Niagara had been thrust into Johnson's lap after Prideaux's death. The frontier leader had no formal military experience and had only been in command once before at Lake George. However, he did a splendid job. The French could not sustain the fighting long after the siege was laid. Niagara surrendered to Johnson on July 25, 1759.[139]

The conquest of Niagara was the greatest British victory up to that time on the North American continent.[140] Milton Hamilton considered the victory at Niagara to be the key to the continent.[141] The general public, for the second time, declared Johnson a hero.[142] The Niagara victory

> won the west. General Stanwix could build away at Fort Pitt without worrying about any danger. The French could not get at him, and the tribes were finally convinced that the English would win the war.[143]

The question remains as to what extent the Iroquois Nations and other Indians contributed to the great victory at Niagara? Obviously, approximately 1,000 of the 3,200 troops who fought for the British side were Indian. Without this group, it would have been much harder for the British to win. In fact, it can be stated that without Indian aid, Niagara would not have fallen. This notion can be inferred by a letter to the Board of Trade on June 5, 1760. It states in part;

> My labors have not been in vain, it being concluded on at that time, by a general convention of the Six Nations and their Allies, after many Solicitations and interesting Arguments Suggested to them by me to join us against the Enemy which they did last year to the amount of above a thousand fighting men at Niagara, from whence I sent them home loaden with the spoils of the French.[144]

The previous passage gave credit to the Iroquois Nations for helping to win the Battle of Niagara and suggested that without Indian support, the outcome would have been different.[145] By 1759, the Iroquois Nations and other Indians could detect the direction of the war. It was obvious to the Native

Americans that as long as the British were winning the war, they should be on the winning side. All the expenses put forth to persuade the Indians to side with the British were, therefore, well worth the effort. Sir William realized, at times the Crown would have hoped for stronger support, but believed all expenses incurred helped him convince the Iroquois Nations and other Indians to side with the British. He also freely admitted that Native American support was easier to muster when the British were winning victories. Johnson stated;

> the assistance His Majestys arms have received from the Indians has not answered Expectation or been adequate to the expenses, I must take the liberty to say, it has in a great measure been owing to the ill success of our military operations this way, hence tho the Indians of the Six Nations amongst whom the moneys which have past through my hands have been chiefly confined, have not seconded out Enterprizes so universally as they might have done, yet numbers of them have every campaign joined His Majestys Troops and some or other of them been constantly upon service, however, had the Expense, which hath already accrued served only to prevent the Six Nations as a Body from going over to the French and acting with them against us, which I am vain enough to think I have had some share in preventing, the moneys laid out have not been uselessly expended.[146]

Therefore, Sir William Johnson's influence and persuasion skills were successful in the two major battles in which he participated during the French and Indian War. At Lake George in 1755, and Niagara in 1759, the Iroquois Nations helped him to win victory. In his own words, he reveals that the Iroquois Nations and other Indians fought bravely in every campaign against the French. It must be noted that British victories in 1758 and 1759 and later made the Indians a much more vigorous ally. However, even in the most dismal and low periods of the war, when the French were strongly winning, Sir William managed to keep the Indians neutral and, through his elaborate intelligence system, obtained valuable information on French military plans.

CHAPTER 6

Was Sir William Johnson's Influence Over the Iroquois and other Indians a Major Factor in Winning the French and Indian War?

Sir William Johnson's influence on the Iroquois Nations and other Indians clearly had an impact on the outcome of the French and Indian War. His influence was very noteworthy and can be substantiated by a number of sources. His persuasion techniques, including his rhetorical skills, kept the Iroquois neutral through much of the war and eventually made them a valuable ally to the British. All of this was chronicled in pre-ceeding chapters.

The Indians fought in every major British campaign against the French and proved that the money devoted to securing their assistance was well worthwhile.[1] Even during the darkest periods of the war, when the Six Nations and their allies only remained neutral, the expense to keep them away from French influence was necessary.[2]

Sir William Johnson realized that his success in keeping the Six Nations and other Indian tribes on the British side or neutral was directly proportional to the number of battles the Crown won and on the amount of money spent to persuade the Indians.[3] However, the question remains, how successful was Sir William Johnson? Did his Indian influence really effect the war? What would have happened if Johnson had not lived? These questions will be answered in this final chapter of this volume.

The French and Indian War was influenced by the commitment the Iroquois Nations and other Indians had toward the conflict. France and Britain vied throughout the war for Native American support. This support or lack of it greatly effected the outcome of numerous battles and, ultimately, to some extent, the war itself. Therefore, Sir William Johnson's Indian influence effected the wars outcome. A few examples of Indian support or lack of it will make this fact evident.

At the beginning of the war, General Braddock's expedition against Fort Duquesne was "surprised by an ambuscade of French and Indians."[4] Braddock and much of his army were killed about eight miles from the fort.[5] The British army on July 9, 1755:

> was seized with a panic from the unusual appearance and horrid cries of the savages; they fled in confusion; they were totally defeated with a considerable slaughter, especially of the officers. The General himself, after having five horses killed under him, was mortally wounded; wiping away all errors of his conduct by an honourable death for his country.[6]

General Braddock's army was massacred on the Monongahela River for several reasons. One was his lack of respect and understanding of the wilderness style of fighting. However, his lack of Indian support also made him very vulnerable to ambush. In wilderness terrain Braddock could have used as many as fifty Indians fanning out ahead of his troops but he had only eight.[7] The French, on the other hand, had over six hundred Indians who harassed the British and finally helped in the victory.[8] Lack of native support made Braddock's force an easy target. Support from the Ottawas,

Chippewas, Potawatomis, Mingos and Shawnees helped the French victory.[9]

Sir William Johnson did not take part in the battle at the Monongahela River or, as it is sometimes called, "the battle of the Wilderness." Johnson had been appointed superintendent of northern Indian affairs by Braddock.[10] He did not influence the outcome of the battle because his important conferences with the Iroquois Nations and other natives had only begun at this time. If Johnson's influence had been greater when the war began, Braddock would have had enough Indians to discover the ambush that caused the massacre. The French had Indian support in 1755, and because the British didn't and underestimated the situation, Braddock and his army lost the battle. The Indians were, in this instance and in future engagements, a deciding factor in the outcome of the battle.

Fort Duquesne was finally taken by the British in the fall of 1758 when the Crown was winning the war. British victories made the work of Sir William Johnson easier by this period. In the case of Fort Duquesne, the Indians abandoned the French and became neutral.[11] They realized, after several skirmishes, that victory against the British was in vain. The Native Americans were "willing and disposed to embrace his majesty's most gracious protection."[12] Johnson had numerous conferences after 1756 to influence the Iroquois Nations and other Indians to fight against the French. Indirectly, this influence, combined with British victories, made Fort Duquesne surrender. Brigadier General Forbes stated that the victory obtained for the British Crown a "prodigious tract of fine, rich country and in a manner of reconciliation of the various tribes and nations of Indians to his majesty's government."[13]

By 1757 and 1758, British victories turned the tide of war and made the former French Indians new allies.[14] A letter from Colonel John Bradstreet to General Jeffrey Amherst reveals this fact. As Bradstreet stated;

> The campaign of 1758 in America was very advantageous and very honourable to the English interest.

Louisburgh, St. Johns, Frontenac and Duquesne reduced, remove from our colonies all terror of the Indian incursions, and draw from the French those useful allies.[15]

Before 1757, the Indians were generally not a great factor in British victories. In his victory over the British at Lake George on September 8, 1755, Sir William Johnson's Indian influence did not decide the battle. This was the case even though over 400 Native Americans fought with Johnson at Lake George. In 1755, when Johnson fought the battle, the British were not winning the war, and it was amazing that the famed New Yorker could get a number of Iroquois to side with the Crown. It is further amazing that Johnson kept many Indians neutral during this period.

At Niagara, Sir William Johnson's victory on July 25, 1759 was influenced greatly by the Iroquois Nations support. Approximately one thousand Iroquois Indians followed him from Fort Stanwix to support Brigadier General Prideaux.[16] The Indians gave the British a decided advantage and ultimately made the Crown victorious.

The French at Niagara under Captain Pouchot had six hundred men.[17] Johnson had thirty-three hundred men, including one thousand Iroquois. These Native Americans were very successful and were committed to the British interest.[18] They influenced most of their prisoners to bury the hatchet and side with the Crown.[19] This is another example of the Indian way of siding with the strongest party.[20] It was obvious in 1759, after the many British victories, that the Crown was winning the war.

The Battle of Niagara was the greatest British victory up to that time. It destroyed communication links between Canada and Louisiana.[21] It was, in many ways, as Milton Hamilton stated, the key to the continent.[22]

After Niagara, General Amherst, commander of the British forces in North America, sent General Thomas Gage to supersede Johnson and take command of the forces at Lake

Ontario.[23] Gage was ordered "to descend the St. Lawrence, attack the French posts at the head of the rapids, and hold them if possible for the winter."[24] However, the French had control of the St. Lawrence at the time.[25] Gage had to provide for the safety of Niagara and Oswego and could not engage in further attacks.[26]

Sir William Johnson tried to motivate General Gage to move against the French and follow the orders that Amherst had given him.[27] The New Yorker thought that conquests of LaGalette and La Présentation on the upper St. Lawrence were possible.[28] Gage would not move and preferred to take the very safe course of waiting." Even the ardent enthusiasm of a Johnson could not prevail against the phlegm of a Loudoun, an Abercromby or a Gage."[29]

Johnson shortly prepared for the conquest of Canada. This was to follow the great victory of Quebec on September 18, 1759 in which the British commander Thomas Wolfe, and the French leader Marquis de Montcalm were both killed.[30] Sir William negotiated with the Six Nations to organize a force to accompany the British on their march northward. In a short time, a large number of Indians were ready to follow Johnson.

The Six Nations, by the late 1750's, saw the writing on the wall. They were eager to follow Johnson in a British victory, but had to be provided with food and supplies. Johnson tapped Amherst's war chest for £5,000.[31] This soon was gone and Sir William had to rely on his own funds to get the Iroquois Nations ready for battle.[32]

John Knox's *Journal of the French and Indian War* states that Johnson led a force of over thirteen hundred Indians with him on the march to Canada. [33] A muster taken on August 5, 1760, amounted to thirteen hundred and thirty.[34] These included members of all the Six Nations plus those of many other Indian tribes.[35] The Cayugas and Onondagas sent 284 and 203 members, respectively.[36] The Senecas sent 114, the Oneidas, 60, the Mohawks, 51, and the Tuscarores, 37.[37] Altogether, seventeen Indian nations were represented in the Native

American force which followed Sir William.[38]

Johnson's 1,330 Indians would have been a formidable army. However, it seems that they were not all warriors. Sir William himself mentions far fewer fighting men. The 1,330 most likely included women and children. Johnson stated:

> I yet was able to proceed from Oswego with upwards of 600 Warriors, but as there were nine Severall Nats. and Tribes of Inds. inhabiting ye Country about Montreal consisting of above 800 fighting men previous to our departure I judged it highly necessary to gain them if possible, at least to bring them to a neutrality, being very sensible of the difficultys which an Army had to encounter in their way to Montreal where a few Indians Joined with other troops might act to great advantage.[39]

Therefore, Sir William's force consisted of approximately 600 warriors. Milton Hamilton agrees with this conclusion and states the number of 1,330 chronicled in the early documents included 600 to 700 warriors and a large number of women and children.[40] Knox's *Historical Journal of the Campaigns in North America for the Years 1757, 1758, 1759 and 1760,* is apparently not completely correct. William Stone, in his biography, *The Life and Times of Sir William Johnson* printed in 1860, also mentioned 1,330 Indians, but had not researched thoroughly to determine that they were not all warriors.

Sir William joined General Amherst's army of 10,000 troops. Amherst was one of three commanders who were converging on Canada. The others included William Haviland, who marched from Crown Point, and Governor Murray, who pressed on from Quebec with twenty-two hundred troops.[41] The outcome was an easy British victory. Pierre Francois de Rigaud, Marquis de Vaudreuil, Governor of Canada, surrendered without a shot being fired.[42] Thus, all of Canada was under British control.

Sir William Johnson's Indian allies were influential in the

great victory at Montreal. He led a group of the fiercest fighters ever bred in America.[43] These natives did no damage to the country or its inhabitants.[44] However, by intimidation and a show of strength, they convinced large numbers of French Indians to switch sides and support the British Crown.[45] Also, by the use of Indian intelligence methods, they gave the British valuable information about the French. Obviously, the Iroquois Nations and other Indians did their part in the Battle of Montreal. Johnson used this good fortune for the British cause. He stated in a letter to William Pitt that his Indians brought:

> us constant Intelligence having none against us, and the Peace which I settled with the 9 Nations before mentioned, was productive of such good Consequence that some of these Indians joined us, whilst the rest preserved so strict a neutrality that we passed all the dangerous Rapids, and the whole way without the least opposition, and by that means came so near to the other two Armies that the Enemy could attempt nothing further without an imminent risque of the City and inhabitants. Thus Sir we became Masters of the last place in the Enemy's possession in these parts and made those Indians our friends by a peace, who might otherwise have given us much trouble.[46]

During the early war years, as stated previously, the British were losing the war and Sir William had trouble influencing the Indians. Later, with the Pitt-Newcastle War ministry in June of 1757, this situation began to change. Pitt was:

> energetic to the point of impatience and, again convinced that France could be humbled by seizing her colonies rather than by facing her huge army on Europe's hard-packed battle fields. To achieve victory, he was not afraid to spend money, thus overcoming the chief colonial objection to co-operation.

Nor was he reluctant to impose his will on the commander in chief in America.[47]

Shortly after William Pitt came into power, the British began to win the war. Due to his energetic leadership and his philosophy of spending, the British began to win major battles. With these victories and with substantial resources, Sir William could persuade the Six Nations to fight with the Crown. From 1757 until the end of the war, Johnson's Iroquois allies were an obvious factor in winning the war. They were a factor in battles in which they took part in, in the elaborate intelligence system that Sir William organized, and in the influence they had on other Indians to join the British side or remain neutral. None of this would have happened without William Pitt coming to power. Therefore, the advent of William Pitt as war minister of the British government allowed Sir William Johnson to influence the Six Nations and ultimately many other Indian tribes to side against France. This influence gave the British a great edge during the last four years of the French and Indian War and was a major factor in the final victory.

The question remains, what would have happened if Sir William Johnson had not lived? Was the work of Sir William that significant? Were there any other British Indian diplomats that could have taken his place?

During Sir William's time, the English had a number of men who were close to the Indians. One of them was John Henry Lydius, who was somewhat of a rival of Johnson's and was employed as an Indian agent by Massachusetts.[48] At first, Lydius seemed friendly to Sir William and appeared to be an honest man.[49] However, as early as 1746, he was thought to be secretly plotting with the French.[50] Johnson shortly realized that Lydius was a shady character who could not be trusted. The Iroquois knew the truth about Lydius. At a council at Mount Johnson, an Oneida sachem named Conochquiesie accused Lydius of cheating them and stealing their lands.[51] The sachem stated to Johnson;

You promised us that you would keep this fireplace clean from all filth and that no snake should come into this Council Room. That man sitting there (pointing to Lydius) is a, and has stole our Lands, he takes Indians slyly by the Blanket one at a time, and when they are drunk, put some money in their Bosoms,and persuades them to sign deeds for our land.[52]

Obviously, John Henry Lydius was not the man to take the place of Sir William Johnson as friend and agent of the Iroquois Nations and other Indians. Johnson made his reputation and fortune by being fair to the Indians. The natives trusted him and felt he was one of them. Lydius, on the other hand, was a common trader of his day. He cheated the Indians whenever he could. The Six Nations and other Indians would never follow his lead against the French. In fact, because of his ties with France, the Indians might even have been persuaded to side with the French over the British.

Conrad Weiser was another contemporary who, like Johnson, had dealings with the Indians. He was from Pennsylvania, but came dashing to New York every time a crisis occurred involving the Iroquois Nations.[53] Weiser was known as an able interpreter and Indian agent, but had little influence on the Six Nations because his base was miles away. Governor William Shirley had mentioned him as a possible successor to Johnson after the Lake George Battle, but this never came about.[54]

Conrad Weiser could have taken over for Johnson because he was a respected diplomat among the Indians. However, he was nearly sixty years old in 1755 and died in 1760. He was too old to have influenced the Iroquois Nations and other Indians as Johnson did. It is doubtful that such an elderly man could have followed the vigorous schedule established by Sir William.

There is another reason why Conrad Weiser would not have been able to influence the Iroquois Nations into a fighting force. He worked for the Quaker government of Pennsylvania, which opposed using Indians for war.[55] Weiser thought "that

Indian allies were expensive and treacherous."[56] He was against Johnson's use of the Iroquois Nations in King George's War and would have never favored large groups of Indians fighting with the British against the French.[57] Although Conrad Weiser was an honest, respected interpreter and diplomat to the Six Nations and other Indians, he was not a Sir William Johnson. If he had charge of the Iroquois, he would most likely have tried to keep them neutral in the last colonial conflict.

George Croghan was another respected Indian trader and diplomat. He was a loyal subordinate to Sir William Johnson. Croghan was from Pennsylvania, and was second only to Johnson in relations with the Pennsylvania tribes and those of the middle west.[58] Croghan was like Sir William, of Irish descent, and began dealing with the Indians in 1741. He soon came into conflict with the French who competed with him for Indian favors.[59]

Sir William Johnson first wrote to George Croghan concerning relations with the Caghnawagas Indians and a chief named Scaroyady. It was Johnson's intention during the early part of the French and Indian War to send Indian aid to General Edward Braddock, who marched toward Fort Duquesne in 1755.[60] Sir William hoped this assistance would come from Pennsylvania Indians and from the Six Nations.[61] Croghan answered Johnson politely and thus began a friendship which lasted many years.[62]

At Mount Johnson, from June 21 to July 4, Sir William held a conference with nine Indian nations.[63] This was shortly after meeting with the Cananjoharies in Albany on June 5.[64] Johnson called upon the Caghnawagas and the Six Nations to join him in the war against the French and George Croghan assured him of his assistance to Braddock.[65] Johnson stated;

> I am appointed to the Chief Command with great guns and other implements of war, to drive the French from their encroachments on your hunting grounds in this Province; if you will be dutiful to the King your Father, if you will be faithful to your

Bretheren the English, if you will treat me as your Brother, Go with me.[66]

Obviously the Caghnawagas never helped Braddock. The Iroquois sent six young braves to join the general, but they were murdered by the French before they reached their destination. After this, Johnson could not persuade the Six Nations to send any more of their people on such a far off journey. The Iroquois Nations felt there were enough friendly southern Indians to the British to help Braddock.[67]

George Croghan was not able to help General Braddock and without Indian aid, the inevitable occurred. Although he was a respected trader and diplomat among the natives, Croghan really did not have the influence Johnson had with the Iroquois Nations and other Indians throughout the latter part of the war. Fifty Caghnawagas would probably have saved Braddock's force from the massacre that occurred. Croghan was not as influential as Sir William Johnson and could not help Braddock. There were many distinct differences between Croghan and Johnson, which also should be mentioned. Croghan, like Johnson, was a sharp trader who was generally trusted by the Indians. However, Croghan could not always keep his diplomacy and speculative ventures separate and lost thousands of pounds when the French and Indian War began. [68] This led to risky and unsound ventures which made him somewhat distrusted on the frontier.[69]

George Croghan was different from Sir William Johnson in other ways. He was a rough frontiersman who did not have the education or ability which Johnson had to deal with all types of people. Although he received the title of Major and then Colonel, he never liked military discipline.[70] He accompanied George Washington and witnessed Braddock's defeat on the Monongahela, but could not influence the Pennsylvania Indians to join the British expedition. A friend of Johnson, he was an honest and capable subordinate.[71] However, he could never have organized the Indians into a fighting force against the French. As for influencing the Six Nations, his base of operation was too many miles away to have had any real influence. Unlike Johnson, he could have never influenced one thousand Iroquois warriors to join the British at Niagara or six-to-seven hundred to accompany Amherst at Montreal. Croghan was a good subordinate, but would not have been able to lead the Office of Indian Service as Johnson did.

Peter Wraxall, who wrote an abridgement of Indian records from 1678-1751, which was used as an early source for this volume, became Secretary of Indian Affairs under Johnson. This was the office he held until his death at the Battle of Niagara on July 11, 1759. His ability as a writer and his loyalty, made him a valuable ally and trusted friend to Sir William Johnson. Devotion to Johnson made him unliked by Sir William's enemies, notably Governor William Shirley.

Wraxall accompanied Johnson at the Battles of Lake George and Niagara, but was not the Indian diplomat or military leader that Sir William was. His early death and rather sickly nature[72] eliminates him as a substitute for the baronet. However, his value to the British and to Johnson cannot be underestimated.

It is very obvious now that there was no British diplomat to the Indians that came up to the stature of Sir William Johnson. No one in colonial history could have done the job of Superintendent of Indian Affairs as well as he. No other diplomat could have organized the Six Nations as a fighting force as well as he did. No one could have influenced the other Indians as much to side with the British or stay neutral in the French and Indian War. Also, no one could have or would have organized a system of Indian intelligence to reveal to the British, French plans in the war.

The French had diplomats that vied for the support of the Iroquois and other nations. The best known and most successful diplomats from France were of the Joncaire family. Louis Thomas de Joncaire (1670-1739) was the elder of the clan.[73] He had a number of sons who followed in his footsteps and were in competition with Sir William Johnson.[74] Johnson's life was in constant danger because of this fact.[75]

Sir William Johnson was not deterred by the constant danger that he faced. He proceeded to confront his French competition at all costs.[76] The Joncaire family realized Johnson's great ability to persuade the Six Nations and other Indians and thus tried to combat his influence.[77] This can be determined from a letter written by Johnson in 1748. The letter discusses a trip Sir William was planning to the Onondaga castle to persuade them not to side with the French and set the tone for the later French and Indian War.[78] The letter states:

> We shall have a fatigueing Journey of it and I reckon pritty dangerous, for I am informed Last Night by Hendricks Son that the French at Cadaraghque haveing heard of it by Jean Cuer (Joncaire) were quite Uneasy att the News and Said they would prevent it wh. is very likely they will attempt it for It would be a thing of great Consequence to them the worst of it is we must march thorough a thick woods for above 100 miles on foot to go thorough all the Castles by the Way In order to talk to some of the most obstinate of them privately. I shall leave no Stone Unturned yu. may depend upon it, to Accomplish wt. I go abt.[79]

Johnson's journey to the Onondagas was successful. He was welcomed graciously with great respect toward the British.[80] The Onondagas did not go to Canada or side with the French at this time. As was the case with the later war, Sir William Johnson's influence won the day.

If Sir William Johnson had not acted in the role of diplomat to the Six Nations and other Indians, the Joncaire family and other French diplomats would have been much more successful. The Senecas sided with the French through much of the French and Indian War. Without Johnson, it is likely that the other tribes would have veered away from neutrality and toward Canada. Two of the Joncaire's were at the surrender of Niagara in 1759. They would have most likely been on the winning side if Johnson had not persuaded over one thousand Iroquois representatives to accompany the British. Obviously, Johnson's influence neutralized the Joncaires. This writer feels no other British diplomat was of the stature of Sir William Johnson. There was no other Indian agent that could have taken his place on this matter and been successful.

The service of Sir William Johnson to the British Crown was enormous. Yet historically he has been neglected in many ways and receives little credit for his influence during the French and Indian War. This volume challenges this belief and asserts that Sir William's influence was immeasurable. One wonders why Sir William Johnson has not been given the credit he deserves. Why have the Indians not been considered a major factor in the outcome of the war? The reasons for these facts are very numerous.

Sir William Johnson was a British official, but he was also Irish. He advanced Irishmen whenever he could. Johnson's Irish background made the British overlook his accomplishments. They made him a baronet, but never trusted him enough to give him command of a major battle. "Gentleman's Magazine" of London applauded his ability to influence the Indians, but never gave him full recognition as a military leader. [81] The British looked down upon Johnson because he was a squaw man who had no shame in bringing halfbreed children into the world.[82]

American history also pays little heed to the memory of Sir William because of obvious reasons. Johnson died in 1774 on the eve of the American Revolution. During the pre-war period, he favored the British side over the American colonists. After his death, "his son, his nephew and many of his descendants took the field against the Revolution."[83] Johnson and his family were considered the enemy and thus, have not been given credit for the services that they performed against France. Also, because of Johnson's influence, the Iroquois sided with the British during the Revolutionary War and were eventually chastised by the order of General George Washington.

Another reason why Sir William Johnson has been neglected in American history is that much of the early history was written by historians from Massachusetts. The pious leaders of the colony looked harshly on the wealthy Irishmen who cohabited with numerous Native American women and yet bypassed typical marriage ceremonies. The long quarrel with Governor Shirley also added to Johnson's lack of acceptance in Massachusetts.[84]

Sir William Johnson obviously has not been significantly eulogized in American history. His private life was an open book and too unorthodox to make him a household word. His great services during the French and Indian War have largely gone unnoticed. His great influence on the Iroquois Nations and other Indians have been passed over by many chroniclers. The noted historian, Francis Parkman, looked harshly on Johnson. Many other writers have accepted Parkman's prejudices.[85]

Sir William Johnson, therefore, has remained largely unknown to Americans in general. Those that have heard of him, have misunderstood his value in the history of our nation. He has not been given the credit he richly deserves. Johnson helped change history by influencing the Iroquois to fight with the British or stay neutral. In actuality, Sir William Johnson was a hero in history.[86]

> The hero in history is the individual to whom we can justifiably attribute preponderant influence in determining an issue or even whose consequences would have been profoundly different if he had not acted as he did.[87]

He was an event-making man who increased the odds for success by the alternative he chose and the extraordinary qualities he possessed.[88]

Johnson left his positive imprint on Colonial American history through his actions. He led an army of the fiercest fighters ever to be born in America.[89] He was not formally trained as an officer, but twice took a French commander as his prisoner.[90] When he took Niagara in 1759, he broke communication between Canada and Louisiana and thus broke the backbone of French resistance.[91] Along with Wolfe and Amherst and the war policies of William Pitt, his services were immeasurable in winning the war. Johnson accomplished this end without once plundering the countryside or injuring civilians.[92]

During the darkest years of the war, when the British were losing, Johnson was hardly able to keep the Iroquois and their allies neutral. This was a great accomplishment by itself. However, with the advent of William Pitt and with the beginning of British victories, things began to change. Thus, Sir William Johnson was able to use his diplomatic ability to persuade the Iroquois. He directly influenced the outcome of the French and Indian War. As he stated in a letter to General Jeffrey Amherst just before the Battle of Niagara:

> Not only from the public and general Declarations of the Indians at this Meeting, but from private conferences I have had with their Chiefs, and a variety of other concurring Circumstances, I think, I have a good foundation to give it as my Opinion to Your Excellency, that, not only from Commencement of the present War, but for many Years past, His Majesty's Indian Interest, hath not Wore so favorable a Face, nor given Us such Encouraging prospects; And that if a Respectable Body of His Majesty's Forces should speedily March towards Lake Ontario, in order to Carry on Operations from thence against the Enemy, I would Join them with the Main Body of the Five Nations and many of their Allies, And that by the Appearance of Our Troops, and taking other Corresponding Measures, I could Succeed in prevailing on those of the Five Nations, who live at LaGallette, to Abandon the French Interest, as well as many Other Nations of Indians to the Northward and Westward, whom the French Expect will Join them.[93]

CONCLUSIONS

In 1745, only seven years after William Johnson had come to colonial New York, he had developed a successful business and was a man of means. He had also become knowledgeable in the ways of the Iroquois Nations. He had learned their languages, traded with them, and became their friend.

Very early on, William Johnson showed his admiration, respect, and understanding for the Six Nations and Indians in general. He spent time learning the language and culture of the Mohawks who lived in his geographic area, near present day Schenectady. While other white traders hated and cheated the Indians, Johnson treated them fairly. He took part in their sports, joined with them in their festivals, and even cohabited with their women. He fathered at least eight children with Native American women, but recognized and provided for them in his will. He showed respect for both the Indian and white races and, in turn, became wealthy through his fair treatment of Native Americans. He also gained tremendous admiration from his Indian neighbors and, ultimately, considerable influence in controlling these Native Americans during the two remaining colonial wars.

Johnson's first public office was as Justice of the Peace in 1745 and, a year later, he was selected to supply the Oswego garrison. He did this admirably and soon became a favorite of Governor George Clinton of New York. He became colonel of the Six Nations of Iroquois in 1746 and slowly became the most respected and influential white man among the Indians.

By 1747, he was sending out war parties regularly to attack small groups in New France.

Johnson lived a dangerous life during the war years. However, by the war's end, his destiny was set. He had done what many thought to be impossible by convincing many Mohawks and other Iroquois Nations to side with the British. He worked hard to keep others neutral. He was so successful that the French wanted him dead or alive. It seemed that his fairness as a trader and merchant, and his liberal feelings about the Native Americans, made the Indians trust him above all other white men. He used this talent to help influence the third colonial war. However, it must be remembered that the only large confrontation between France and Britain in America during that war was at Louisbourg. Johnson did not take part in that action.

In the last conflict between France and Britain, William Johnson's Indian philosophy, his fairness, and his ability at persuasion, helped to influence and change history. He conducted over forty-five conferences with the Indians during the French and Indian War to convince the Iroquois Nations and their allies to fight against the French. He showed tremendous vigor, for many times, his life was in danger as he travelled into French-occupied territory. During the early part of the war, Johnson was fortunate to keep the Indians neutral. This was because the French were winning the war at this time.

In 1757, William Pitt took charge of the war effort between Britain and France. He began to pump money into the conflict. Pitt's philosophy was to try to win the war in North America and thus beat France once and for all. Shortly, the British began to win battles against the French.

Sir William Johnson won two major battles for the British Crown. On September 8, 1755, he won the Battle of Lake George. At this battle, he captured the French commander, Baron Dieskau. He treated this leader admirably and protected him against hostilities of the Iroquois. As a result of the Lake George battle, Johnson was made a baronet.

In 1759, Sir William Johnson led one thousand Iroquois warriors at the Battle of Niagara under the command of John Prideaux. Prideaux was killed before the engagement began and Johnson took over command with vigor. The French surrendered to him on July 25 after being besieged by the British force. The French expected reinforcements, but these were ambushed by a force sent out by Johnson. In this case, Sir William's elaborate Indian intelligence system gave him valuable information that helped the outcome of a major battle.

The conquest of Niagara was the greatest British victory during the French and Indian War up to that time in 1759. Milton Hamilton, an acknowledged authority on Sir William Johnson, considered it the key to the continent. It cut the line of communication between Canada and Louisiana. It was the beginning of the end for France.

In September, 1760, Sir William Johnson led a force of over thirteen hundred Indians, of which approximately six to seven hundred were warriors, to join General Jeffrey Amherst in the capture of Montreal. Montreal and all of Canada fell on September 8. Johnson's Indian warriors definitely effected this outcome.

The influence that Sir William Johnson had on the Iroquois Nations and other Indians resulted in the Six Nations taking part in every major engagement against the French. In battles such as the Battle of the Wilderness, in which General William Braddock and his whole force were massacred, only eight Indians accompanied the British. In battles when large numbers of Iroquois representatives participated in battles, such as Lake George and Niagara and later Montreal, the British were victorious.

Sir William Johnson's influence over the Iroquois Nations also resulted in other Indian groups, some of which were allies of the French, to change sides. The Iroquois Confederation were very intimidating to other Indians. After 1757, when it was obvious that the British were winning the war, they put pressure on their allies and other Indians to fight with the British. This resulted in many Nations changing sides and joining the Crown.

Sir William Johnson was not the only Indian diplomat that worked among the Iroquois Nations. However, no other individual had the stature of Johnson. No one else could have influenced the Iroquois Nations the way he did. If his influence had not occurred, the French diplomats such as the Joncaires would have been much more successful. Therefore, Sir William Johnson's influence over the Iroquois Nations and other Indians definitely influenced the French and Indian War. Johnson, by his actions, effectively changed the outcome of American history. However, he has not been given the credit for his actions. Sir William Johnson was a giant in colonial American history. Hopefully, future accounts will elevate him to the rightful place he so richly deserves.

FOOTNOTES

CHAPTER 1

1. *The Johnson Papers*, Albany: The University of the State of New York., 1921, Volume I, Introduction, Genealogy Section, p. XXXV.

2. Ibid.

3. Milton W. Hamilton, *Sir William Johnson Colonial American 1715-1763*, Port Washington, New York: Kennikat Press., 1976, p. 4.

4. Ibid. p. 5

5. Samuel Madden, *Reflections and Resolutions Proper for the Gentlemen of Ireland, As to their Conduct for the Service of their Company,* Dublin: R. Reilly., 1738., p. 11.

6. Ibid.

7. Ibid.

8. Ibid., p. 27.

9. Ibid.

10. *The Johnson Papers*, Albany: The University of the State of New York., 1921, Volume I, Introduction, Genealogy, Section, p. XXXIV.

11. Milton W. Hamilton, *Sir William Johnson Colonial American 1715-1763*, Port Washington, New York: Kennikat Press., 1976, p. 4.

12. Arthur Young, *A Tour in Ireland with General Observations on the Present State of that Kingdom made in the Years 1776, 1777, 1778, and 1779*, Dublin: George Bohham, 1780., p. 79.

13. Ibid.

14. Ibid.

15. Ibid.

16. Ibid., p. 71.

17. Ibid.

18. Milton W. Hamilton, *Sir William Johnson Colonial American 1715-1763*, Port Washington, New York: Kennikat Press., 1976, p. 5.

19. *Johnson Papers*, Albany: The University of the State of New York., 1921., Volume XIII, p. 1071. (footnotes) Also Franz V. Recum, Families of Warren and Johnson of Warrenstown, County Meath, Ireland, New York: The New York Historical Society, 1950., and

20. Milton W. Hamilton, *Sir William Johnson Colonial American 1715-1763*, Port Washington, New York: Kennikat Press., 1976, p. 334 (footnotes).

21. Edith Mead Fox, *William Johnson's Early Career as a Frontier Landlord and Trader*, Ithaca, New York, (M.A. Thesis at Cornell University), 1945., p. 2.

22. Arthur Young, *A Tour in Ireland with General Observations on the Present State of that Kingdom made in the Years 1776, 1777, 1778, and 1779*, p. 43.

23. Edith Mead Fox, *William Johnson's Early Career as a Frontier Landlord and Trader*, p. 3.

24. George T. Stokes ed., *Pococke's Tour in Ireland in 1752*, Dublin: Hodges, Figgis and Company., 1891., p. 177.

25. James Thomas Flexner, *Lord of the Mohawks: A Biography of Sir William Johnson*, Boston: Little Brown and Company, 1959., p. 10.

26. Milton W. Hamilton, *Sir William Johnson Colonial American 1715-1763*, p. 5.

27. Ibid. p. 6.

28. *Johnson Papers*, Volume 1, p. 907.

29. Ibid.

30. Milton W. Hamilton, *Sir William Johnson Colonial American 1715-1763*, (footnotes) p. 334.

31. William Maxwell Reid, *The Story of Old Fort Johnson*, New York: G. P. Putnam and Sons, 1906., p. 4.

32. Ibid. 5.

33. Arthur Pound, *Johnson of the Mohawks: A Biography of Sir William Johnson*, New York: The Macmillan Company, 1930., p. 28.

34. Ibid.

35. Ibid., pp. 28-29.

36. Ibid., p. 28

37. Augustine Buell, *Sir William Johnson*, New York: D. Appleton and Company, 1903., p. 6.

38. Ibid., p. 7.

39. Ibid.

40. Arthur Pound, *Johnson of the Mohawks: A Biography of Sir William Johnson*, New York: The Macmillan Company, 1930., p. 27.

41. Augustine Buell, *Sir William Johnson*, New York: D. Appleton and Company, 1903., p. 7.

42. Ibid.

43. Ibid., pp. 7-8.

44. Franz vonRecum, *The Families of Warren and Johnson of Warrenstown, County Meath, Ireland*, New York: The New York Historical Society, 1950., p. 3.

45. *Johnson Papers*, Albany: The University of the State of New York., 1921, Volume I, Introduction, Genealogy Section, p. XXXV.

46. Edward Bailey O'Callaghan ed., *Documents Relative to the State of New York, Calwallader Calden Papers* (A letter to Calden by Dan Hormanden), Albany: Weed, Parsons, and Company Printers, 1856., Volume I, p. 153.

47. Ibid.

48. *Johnson Papers*, Albany: the University of the State of New York., 1921, Volume I, Introduction, Genealogy, p. XVII.

49. Ibid., Volume 13, pp. 28-33.

50. Milton W. Hamilton, *Sir William Johnson Colonial American 1715-1763*, p. 8 and p. 334 (footnotes).

51. William Maxwell Reid, *The Story of Old Fort Johnson*, New York: G. P. Putnam and Sons, 1906., p. 7.

52. Augustine Buell, *Sir William Johnson*, New York: D. Appleton and Company, 1903., p. 9.

53. Ibid., p. 10.

54. Milton W. Hamilton, *Sir William Johnson Colonial American 1715-1763.*, pp. 8-10 and p. 334.

55. James Thomas Flexner, *Lord of the Mohawks: A Biography of Sir William Johnson*, pp. 13-16.

56. Milton W. Hamilton, *Sir William Johnson Colonial American 1715-1763.*, p. 8.

57. Augustine Buell, *Sir William Johnson*, p. 9.

58. Milton W. Hamilton, *Sir William Johnson Colonial American 1715-1763*, p. 8 and p. 334. Also map by Robert Treat Paine 1755, Massachusetts Historical Society, printed in the bulletin of the Fort Ticonderoga Museum 10 number 4 February 1960, p. 263. The map shows an overland route was probable between Albany and Boston

during William Johnson's time and that this was the route he must have taken. I agree with Dr. Hamilton that Johnson took this route.

59. Adolph B. Benson ed. Peter Kalm's *Travels In North America., The America of 1750*, New York: Wilson-Erickson Inc., 1937., pp. 340-342.

60. Ibid., pp. 343. Also: Milton W. Hamilton, *Sir William Johnson Colonial American 1715-1763.*, pp. 9-10.

61. Augustine Buell, *Sir William Johnson*, New York: D. Appleton and Company, 1903., p. 12.

62. Ibid.

63. *Johnson Papers*, Albany: The University of the State of New York., 1921-1965, Volume IX., p. 1.

64. Ibid.

65. Ibid., Volume I, p. 7.

66. Ibid.

67. Augustine Buell, *Sir William Johnson.*, p. 13.

68. Ibid.

69. *Johnson Papers*, Volume I., pp. 4-5.

70. William Maxwell Reid, *The Story of Old Fort Johnson*, p. 9.

71. Augustine Buell, *Sir William Johnson*, p. 13.

72. *Johnson Papers* Volume I., p. 5.

73. Ibid., pp. 5-6.

74. Augustine Buell, *Sir William Johnson*, p. 12.

75. Ibid.

76. *Johnson Papers*, Volume I., p. 31.

77. Ibid., p. 32.

78. Milton W. Hamilton, "*William Johnson's Wives*", New York History, XXXVIII, January, 1957., p. 22.

79. Milton W. Hamilton, *Sir William Johnson Colonial American 1715-1763*, p. 33.

80. William Maxwell Reid, *The Story of Old Fort Johnson*, pp. 19-20.

81. Milton W. Hamilton, "*William Johnson's Wives*", New York History, p. 24.

82. Ibid. Also *Johnson Papers*, Volume 13., William Johnson's Will, pp. 1068-1070.

83. Milton W. Hamilton, "*William Johnson's Wives*", p. 25.

CHAPTER 2

1. Caldwalder Colden, *The History of the Five Nations of Canada*, London: Lockyer Davis, 1755., Volume I., pp. 1-2.

2. Ibid., p. 1, also Paul A. W. Wallace, *The White Roots of Peace,* Philadelphia: The University of Pennsylvania Press, 1946., p. 3.

3. Paul A. W. Wallace, *The White Roots of Peace,* p. 3.

4. Caldwalder Colden, *The History of the Five Nations of Canada*, p. 5.

5. Ibid.

6. Ibid.

7. Paul A. W. Wallace, *The White Roots of Peace*, p.3.

8. William Ritchie, *The Indian History of New York State*, Volume 2, The Iroquoian Tribes, Albany, 1953., p. 14.

9. David M. Ellis, James A. Frost, and Harry F. Carman, *A Short History of New York*, Ithaca, New York: Cornell University Press, 1962., p. 12.

10. David Cusick, *Sketches of Ancient History of the Six Nations*, Tuscarora Village: Lewiston, Niagara Company, 1828., p. 5.

11. George T. Hunt, *The Wars of The Iroquois*, Madison: The University of Wisconsin Press, 1940., p. 67.

12. Paul A. W. Wallace, *The White Roots of Peace*, pp. 3-4.

13. Ibid.

14. Lewis H. Morgan, *Ho Dè-No-Saù Nee or the League of the Iroquois*, New York: Dodd, Mead and Company, 1901., p. 191.

15. Ibid.

16. Ibid.

17. George T. Hunt, *The Wars of the Iroquois*, p. 68.

18. Ibid., p. 69.

19. Ibid.

20. Ibid.

21. Ibid., p. 81.

22. Ibid., p. 82.

23. Ibid.

24. Edward B. O'Callaghan ed. *The Documentary History of the State of New York Albany*: Weed Parsons and Company Publishers, 1849., Volume I., p. 154.

25. Ibid.

26. Ibid.

27. Lawrence H. Lder ed. *The Robert Livington Indian Records 1666-1723, Gettysburg Pennsylvania: The Pennsylvania Historical Association*, 1956., Introduction by Paul A. W. Wallace, T*he Iroquois: A Brief Outline of their History*, p. 18.

28. Ibid.

29. Ibid.

30. Ibid.

31. Ibid.

32. Ibid.

33. Ibid.

34. Ibid., p. 21.

35. Edward B. O'Callaghan ed. T*he Documentary History of the State of New York,* Volume I, p. 133.

36. Ibid.

37. Ibid.

38. Lawrence H, Lder ed. *The Robert Livington Indian Records 1666-1723*, Gettysburg, Pennsylvania: The Pennsylvania Historical Association, 1956., p. 151.

39. Ibid.

40. Lewis H. Morgan., *Ho-Dè=No-Saù-Nee or the League of the Iroquois*, p. 193.

41. Edward B. O'Callaghan ed. *Documents Relative to the State of New York*, Albany: Weed, Parsons and Company Printers, 1856., Volume III., p. 255.

42. Caldwalder Colden, *The History of the Five Nations of Canada*, Volume I., p. 108. Also Lewis H. Morgan, *The League of the Iroquois*, p. 193.

43. George T. Hunt, *The Wars of the Iroquois*, p. 69.

44. Milton W. Hamilton, Sir William Hamilton, *Colonial American 1715-1763*, Port Washington, New York: Kennikat Press, 1976., p. 336 (footnotes).

45. Anthony F. C. Wallace, "*Origins of Iroquois Neutrality: The Grand Settlement of 1701*", *Pennsylvania History, XXIV, July 1957.*, pp. 223-235.

46. Ibid.

47. Charles Howard McIlwain ed., *An Abridgement of the Indian Affairs Contained in Four Folio Volumes, Translated in the Colony of New York, from the Year 1678-to the Year 1751, by Peter Wraxall*, New York and London: Benjamin Blom, 1968., pp. 82-86.

48. Ibid., p. 82.

49. Ibid.

50. Ibid., p. 83.

51. Ibid., pp. 84-85.

52. Ibid., p. 85

53. Ibid.

54. Daniel Richter, "*Cultural Brokers and Intercultural Politics: New York Iroquois Relations 1664-1701*", The Journal of American History, LXXV, June, 1988., p. 41

55. Ibid.

56. Ibid.

57. Ibid. Also Anthony F. C. Wallace, "*The Origins of Iroquois Neutrality: The Grand Settlement of 1701*", *Pennsylvania History*, pp. 223-235.

58. Lewis H. Morgan, *Ho-Dè-No-Saù-Nee or the League of the Iroquois*, p. 194.

59. *The Sir William Johnson Papers*, Prepared for publication by the Division of Archives and History, Albany: The University of the State of New York, 1921-1965., Volume 1., p. 59.

60. Ibid.

61. James Thomas Flexner, *Lord of the Mohawks: A Biography of Sir William Johnson*, Boston: Little, Brown and Company, 1979., p. 37.

62. Milton W. Hamilton, *Sir William Johnson Colonial American 1715-1763*, p. 23.

63. Ibid.

64. *The Sir William Johnson Papers*, Volume 1., p. 239.

65. Caldwalder Colden, *The History of the Five Nations of Canada*, Part 3, pp. 42-43.

66. *The Sir William Johnson Papers*, (A Letter from Johnson to James Delancy), Volume 1., p. 560.

67. Ibid.

68. William Leete Stone, *The Life and Times of Sir William Johnson*, Albany: J. Munsell, 1860., Volume I., p. 189.

69. Robert Rogers, *Ponteach: or The Savages of America, A Tragedy*, London: Printed by the author and sold by J. Millan, 1766., p. 4.

70. Ibid., p. 5.

71. Ibid.

72. Ibid., p. 4.

73. Ibid.

74. Howard Doughty, *Francis Parkman*, New York: The Macmillan Company, 1962., p. 374.

75. Peter Lloyd, T*he Emergence of A Racial Prejudice Toward the Indian in Seventeenth Century New England*, A Doctoral Dissertation at Ohio State University, 1975., p. 30.

76. Ibid.

77. Robert Rogers, *Ponteach: or The Savages of America, A Tragedy*, p. 9.

78. Milton W. Hamilton, *"Sir William Johnson's Wives" New York History*, XXXVIII, January, 1957., p. 23.

79. Ibid.

80. Ibid., p. 25.

81. *The Sir William Johnson Papers*, Volume 13., p. 1070.

82. Ibid.

83. Charles Howard McIlwain ed., *An Abridgement of the Indian Affairs Contained in Four Folio Volumes, Translated in the Colony of New York, From the Year 1678 to the Year 1751, by Peter Wraxall*, p. 248.

84. Ibid.

85. Ibid.

86. *The Sir William Johnson Papers*, Volume 1, p. 81.

87. Ibid.

88. Ibid., p. 84.

89. Ibid.

90. Ibid.

91. Edward B. O'Callaghan ed., *The Documentary History of the State of New York*, Volume II., pp. 581-582.

92. Ibid., pp. 580-582.

93. *The Sir William Johnson Papers*, Volume 13., p. 192.

94. Caldwalder Colden, *The History of the Five Nations of Canada*, part 3., p. 164. Also Milton W. Hamilton, Sir William Johnson Colonial American 1715-1763, p. 53.

CHAPTER 3

1. Charles Howard McIlwain ed., *An Abridgement of the Indian Affairs contained in Four Folio Volumes, Translated in the Colony of New York From the Year 1678- to the Year 1751*, by Peter Wraxall, New York and London: Benjamin Blom, 1968., p. 232.

2. Caldwalder Colden, *The History of the Five Nations of Canada,* London: Lockeyer Davis, 1755., preface to Part 2, p. 3.

3. George Laurence Gomme ed., *"The Gentleman's Magazine – Topographical History 1731-1868",* London: E. Stock, 1756, Volume 26., p. 404.

4. Ibid.

5. Ibid.

6. Ibid.

7. Charles Howard McIlwain ed., *An Abridgement of the Indian Affairs contained in Four Folio Volumes, Translated in the Colony of New York From the Year 1678- to the Year 1751,* by Peter Wraxall, p. 231.

8. Ibid.

9. Augustine Buell, *Sir William Johnson,* New York: D. Appleton and Company, 1903., p. 31.

10. Ibid.

11. Ibid.

12. Ibid.

13. Ibid.

14. Ibid.

15. *The Sir William Johnson Papers,* Albany: The University of the State of New York., 1921-1965, Volume IX, p. 3.

16. Ibid.

17. Ibid.

18. Milton W. Hamilton, *Sir William Johnson Colonial American 1715-1763,* Port Washington, New York: Kennikat Press., 1976, p. 322.

19. Ibid.

20. Augustine Buell, *Sir William Johnson,* p. 31.

21. *The Sir William Johnson Papers,* Volume I, pp. 22-23.

22. Ibid., p. 22

23. Ibid., p. 23

24. Ibid.

25. Edward Bailey O'Callaghan ed., *Documents Relative to the State of New York,* Albany: Weed, Parsons and Company Printers, 1856., Volume VI., p. 268.

Also:

Milton W. Hamilton, *Sir William Johnson Colonial American 1715-1763,* p. 43.

26. Ibid., *Documents Relative to the State of New York*, Volume VI., pp. 249-250.

27. *The Sir William Johnson Papers*, Volume I., p. XVII, introduction.

28. *The Letters and Papers of Caldwalder Colden*, New York: Printed for the New York State Historical Society, Volume IX, 1937., p. 20.

29. Ibid., p. 21

30. Ibid.

31. Stanley Nider Katz ed. *Newcastle's New York: Anglo-American Politics 1732-1753*, Cambridge, Massachusetts: Belkap Press of Harvard University Press, 1968., p. 179.

32. Ibid.

33. Ibid.

34. *Sir William Johnson Papers*, Volume I., pp. 70-71.

35. Ibid.

36. Ibid., p. 49.

37. *The Sir William Johnson Papers*, Volume IX., pp. 32-33.

38. Ibid.

39. Ibid., p. 32.

40. *The Sir William Johnson Papers*, Volume I., p. XVII, Introduction.

41. Ibid.

42. William Maxwell Reid, *The Story of Old Fort Johnson*, New York: G.P. Putnam and Sons, 1906., p. 11.

43. Ibid.

44. Ibid.

45. *The Sir William Johnson Papers*, Volume IX., p. 4

Also:

Milton W. Hamilton, *Sir William Johnson Colonial American 1715-1763*, p. 52.

46. *The Sir William Johnson Papers*, Volume IX, p. 4.

47. Flora Warren Seymour, *Lords of the Valley: Sir William Johnson and his Mohawk Brothers*, London and New York: Longmans, Green and Company, 1930., p. 78.

48. Ibid.

49. Edward Bailey O'Callaghan ed., *Documents Relative to the State of New York*, Volume XI., p. 343.

50. Ibid.

51. Ibid.

52. Flora Warren Seymour, Lords of the Valley: *Sir William Johnson and His Mohawk Brothers*, p. 29.

53. Ibid.

54. Ibid.

55. Herbert L. Osgood, *The American Colonies in the Eighteenth Century*, New York: Columbia University Press, Volume III, 1924., p. 515.

56. Ibid.

57. Ibid., p. 516.

58. William Leete Stone, *The Life and Times of Sir William Johnson*, Albany: J. Munsell, 1860., Volume I., p. 190.

59. *The Letters and Papers of Caldwalder Colden, Volume IX.*, p. 33.

60. Ibid., p. 34.

61. *The Sir William Johnson Papers*, Volume I., p. 42.

62. Ibid., p. 43.

63. Ibid.

64. Ibid.

65. Charles Howard McIlwain ed., *An Abridgement of the Indian Affairs contained in Four Folio Volumes, Translated in the Colony of New York from the Year 1678- to the Year 1751* by Peter Wraxall, p. 246.

66. Milton W. Hamilton, *Sir William Johnson Colonial American 1715-1763*, p. 52.

67. *The Sir William Johnson Papers*, Volume I., p. XVIII, Introduction.

68. Charles Howard McIlwain ed., *An Abridgement of the Indian Affairs contained in Four Folio Volumes, Translated in the Colony of New York From the Year 1678– to the Year 1751*, by Peter Wraxall, p. 247.

69. Ibid., pp. 247-248.

70. Ibid.

71. Ibid.

72. James Thomas Flexner, *Lord of the Mohawks: A Biography of Sir William Johnson*, Boston: Little, Brown and Company, 1979., pp. 37-40.

73. Milton W. Hamilton, *Sir William Johnson Colonial American 1715-1763*, p. 342 (footnotes).

74. Ibid.

75. Ibid.

76. William Leete Stone, *The Life and Times of Sir William Johnson*, p. 190.

77. Ibid.

78. Ibid., pp. 190-191.

79. *The Letters and Papers of Caldwalder Colden*, Volume IX., p. 23.

80. Ibid.

81. Ibid.

82. *The Sir William Johnson Papers*, Volume I., pp. 60-61.

83. Ibid.

84. Ibid.

85. Ibid.

86. Ibid., p. 84.

87. Ibid., p. XVII, Introduction.

88. Ibid.

89. Ibid., p. 119.

90. Ibid., pp. 117-118.

91. Ibid.

92. Ibid., p. 118.

93. Ibid., p. XVIII, Introduction.

94. Ibid.

95. Edward B. O'Callaghan ed., *The Documentary History of the State of New York Albany:* Weed Parsons and Company Publishers, 1849., Volume II., p. 618.

96. Edward B. O'Callaghan ed., *The Documents Relative to the State of New York*, Volume VI, p. 379.

97. Ibid., p. 396.

98. Ibid., p. 628.

99. *The Sir William Johnson Papers*, Volume I., p. XVIII, Introduction.

100. Ibid.

101. Ibid., pp. 160-162.

102. Ibid., p. 159.

103. Ibid., pp. 161-162.

104. Ibid., p. 162.

105. Ibid.

106. Ibid., p. 260.

107. Ibid., p. 261.

108. Charles Howard McIlwain ed., *An Abridgement of the Indian Affairs contained in Four Folio Volumes, Translated in the Colony of New York From the Year 1678- to the Year 1751*, by Peter Wraxall, p. 247.

CHAPTER 4

1. George Laurence Gomme ed., "The Gentleman's Magazine - Topographical History 1731-1868", London: E. Stock, 1756, Volume 26., p. 404.

2. Charles Howard McIlwain ed., A *Abridgement of the Indian Affairs contained in Four Folio Volumes, Translated in the Colony of New York From the Year 1678 - to the Year 1751*, by Peter Wraxall, New York and London: Benjamin Blom, 1968, p. 247.

3. Ibid.

4. *The Sir William Johnson Papers*, Albany: The University of the State of New York., 1921-1965, volume IX, p. 35.

5. Ibid.

6. Ibid., pp. 43-45.

7. Ibid

8. Ibid., p. 43.

9. Ibid., pp. 43-44.

10. Ibid., pp. 43-45.

11. *The Sir William Johnson Papers*, Albany: The University of the State of New York., 1921-1965, Volume I, p. XVII, introduction.

12. Ibid.

13. William Maxwell Reid, *The Story of Old Fort Johnson*, New York: G.P. Putnam and Sons, 1906., p. 9.

14. Milton W. Hamilton, *Sir William Johnson Colonial American 1715-1763*, Port Washington, New York: The Kennikat Press., 1976., p. 69.

15. *The Sir William Johnson Papers*, Volume I, pp. 238-240.

16. Ibid., pp. 238-239.

17. Ibid., p. 239.

18. *The Sir William Johnson Papers*, Volume IX, p. 44.

19. Ibid.

20. Ibid.

21. *The Sir William Johnson Papers*, Volume I., pp. XVII-XIX, introduction.

22. Ibid., p. XIX.

23. Ibid.

24. Augustus Buell, *Sir William Johnson*, New York: D. Appleton and Company, 1903., p. 74.

25. Ibid.

26. Ibid.

27. Ibid., p. 75.

28. Ibid., p. 76.

29. *The Sir William Johnson Papers*, Volume I, p. 342., Also p. XIX, introduction.

30. Ibid., pp. 342-343.

31. Ibid., p. 339.

32. Ibid., p. 340

33. Ibid.

34. Ibid., p. 341.

35. *The Sir William Johnson Papers*, Volume IX, p. 44.

36. James Thomas Flexner, *Lord of the Mohawks: A Biography of Sir William Johnson*, Boston: Little Brown and Company, 1979., pp. 75-77.

37. Milton W. Hamilton, *Sir William Johnson Colonial American 1715-1763,* p. 80

38. *The Sir William Johnson Papers*, Volume I, p. 314.

39. Ibid., p. XIX, introduction.

40. Ibid., pp. 356-357.

41. Ibid., p. 370.

42. Ibid.

43. Ibid.

44. Ibid., p. XIX, introduction.

45. Ibid.

46. Ibid.

47. Ibid.

48. Edward Bailey O'Callaghan ed., *The Documentary History of the State of New York*, Albany: Weed Parsons and Company Publishers, 1849., Volume III., p. 630.

49. Edward Bailey O'Callaghan ed., *Documents Relative to the State of New York*, Albany: Weed Parsons and Company Publishers, 1856., Volume VI., p. 797.

50. Ibid.

51. Richard B. Morris ed., *Encyclopedia of American History, New York:* Harper and Row Publishers, 1965., pp. 65-66.

52. *The Sir William Johnson Papers*, Volume I, p. 406.

53. Ibid.

54. William Livington ed., *Review of the Military Operations in North America; From the Commencement of the French Hostilities on the Frontiers of Virginia in 1753, to the Surrender of Oswego on the 14th of August, 1756*, Dublin: Printed for P. Wilson, and J. Exshaw., 1757., p. 19

55. Augustus Buell, *Sir William Johnson*, p. 89.

56. Ibid.

57. William Livington ed., *Review of the Military Operations in North America; From the Commencement of the French Hostilities on the Frontiers of Virginia in 1753, to the Surrender of Oswego on the 14th of August, 1756*, p. 19

58. Ibid.

59. Ibid.

60. Ibid.

61. Ibid.

62. Ibid., pp. 20-21.

63. Ibid.

64. Ibid.

65. Edward Bailey O'Callaghan ed., *Documents Relative to the State of New York*, Albany: Weed, Parsons and Company Publishers, 1856., Volume VI., pp. 897-899.

66. Ibid.

67. Milton W. Hamilton, *Sir William Johnson Colonial American 1715-1763*, p. 110.

68. *The Sir William Johnson Papers*, Volume IX, pp. 151-152.

Also Milton W. Hamilton, *Sir William Johnson Colonial American 1715-1763*, p. 112.

69. William Livington ed., *Review of the Military Operations in North America; From the Commencement of the French Hostilities on the Frontiers of Virginia in 1753, to the Surrender of Oswego on the 14th of*

August, 1756, Dublin: Printed for P. Wilson, and J. Exshaw., 1756., p. 22.

70. Augustus Buell, *Sir William Johnson* , p. 91.

71. Ibid.

72. George Laurence Gomme ed., "The Gentleman's Magazine - Topographical History 1731-1868", London: E. Stock, 1756, Volume 26., p. 268.

73. *The Sir William Johnson Papers*, Volume I, p. 404.

74. Ibid., p. XX, introduction.

75. Ibid.

76. Ibid., pp. 448-449.

77. Ibid., p. XX, introduction.

78. Ibid.

79. Ibid., pp 540-541.

80. Ibid.

81. Charles Henry Lincoln ed., *The Correspondence of William Shirley, Governor of Massachusetts and Military Commander In America*, New York: The Macmillan Company., 1912., Volume I., p. 193.

82. Ibid.

83. Ibid., pp. 194-195.

84. James Thomas Flexner, *Lord of the Mohawks: A Biography of Sir William Johnson*, p. 188.

85. Ibid.

86. An *Account of Conferences held and Treaties made between Major-General Sir William Johnson Bart and the Chief Sachems and Warriors of the Mohawks, Oneidas, Onondagas, Cayugas, Senekas, Tuskaroras, Aughquageys, Skaniadaradighronos, Chugnuts, Mahickanders, Shawanese, Kanuskagos, Toderigaronos and Ogbquagoes*, London: Printed for A. Millar in the Strand, 1756., pp. 3-62.

87. Ibid., pp. 3-5.

88. Ibid., p. 4.

89. Ibid.

90. Ibid.

91. Ibid.

92. *The Sir William Johnson Papers*, Volume I, p. XXI, introduction.

93. *An Account of Conferences held and Treaties made between Major-General Sir William Johnson Bart and the Chief Sachems and Warriors of the Mohawks, Oneidas, Onondagas, Cayugas, Senekas, Tuskaroras,*

Aughquageys, Skaniadaradighronos, Chugnuts, Mahickanders, Shawanese, Kanuskagos, Toderigaronos and Ogbquagoes, p. 4.

94. Ibid., p. 5.

95. Ibid.

96. Ibid.

97. Ibid.

98. Ibid., p. 6.

99. Ibid., p. 7.

100. Ibid.

101. Ibid., p. 18

102. Ibid.

103. Ibid.

104. Ibid., p. 22.

105. Ibid.

106. Ibid.

107. *The Sir William Johnson Papers*, Volume I, p. 434.

Also Edward Bailey O'Callaghan ed., *Documents Relative to the State of New York*, Volume VII., p. 35.

108. Ibid.

109. *An Account of Conferences held and Treaties made between Major-General Sir William Johnson Bart and the Chief Sachems and Warriors of the Mohawks, Oneidas, Onondagas, Cayugas, Senekas, Tuskaroras, Aughquageys, Skaniadaradighronos, Chugnuts, Mahickanders, Shawanese, Kanuskagos, Toderigaronos and Ogbquagoes,* pp. 23-24.

110. Ibid., p. 25.

111. Ibid.

112. Ibid.

113. Ibid., p. 29

114. Ibid.

115. Ibid., p. 24.

116. Ibid., pp. 25-26.

117. Ibid., pp. 61-62.

118. Ibid., p. 55.

119. *The Sir William Johnson Papers*, Volume I, pp. XIX-XXVIII, introduction.

120. *An Account of Conferences held and Treaties made between Major-General Sir William Johnson Bart and the Chief Sachems and Warriors of the Mohawks, Oneidas, Onondagas, Cayugas, Senekas, Tuskaroras, Aughquageys, Skaniadaradighronos, Chugnuts, Mahickanders, Shawanese, Kanuskagos, Toderigaronos and Ogbquagoes,* pp. 29-46.

121. James Thomas Flexner, *Lord of the Mohawks: A Biography of Sir William Johnson,* pp. 225-226.

122. Ibid., p. 226.

123. Ibid., p. 99.

124. Milton W. Hamilton, *"Sir William Johnson's Wives" New York History,* XXXVII, January, 1957., p. 18.

125. Augustus Buell, *Sir William Johnson,* pp. 51-54.

126. Milton W. Hamilton, *"Sir William Johnson's Wives",* New York History, p. 19.

127. Proceedings and Treaties with the Shawanese Nanticokes and Mohikander Indians Living at Otsiningo on one of the West Branches of the Susquehanna River Negotiated at Fort Johnson in the County of Albany in the Province of New York, April 14-23rd 1757 by the Honourable Sir William Johnson Bart Published by Earl of Loudoun, New York: J. Parker and W. Weyman, 1757., p. 6.

128. Ibid., pp. 8-9.

129. Ibid.

130. Ibid.

131. Ibid., pp. 12-13.

132. Ibid., p. 13.

133. *The Sir William Johnson Papers,* Volume I, p. 669,

134. Ibid.

135. Ibid., p. 706.

136. Ibid.

137. Ibid.

CHAPTER 5

1. Francis Parkman. *France and England in North America,* New York: Literary Classics of the United States, Inc., 1983., Volume II, pp. 932-971.

2. Lawrence H. Lder ed. *The Robert Livington Indian Records 1666-1723*, Gettysburg, Pennsylvania: The Pennsylvania Historical Association, 1956., p. 48.

3. Ibid., p. 52.

4. Ibid., p. 51-54.

5. Ibid., p. 52.

6. Francis Parkman. *France and England in North America*, p. 984.

7. Ibid.

8. *The Sir William Johnson Papers*, Albany: The University of the State of New York., 1921-1965, Volume I., pp. 465-466.

9. Ibid.

10. Ibid., p. 540-542.

11. Ibid., p. 505-506.

Also: Milton W. Hamilton. *Sir William Johnson Colonial American 1715-1763*, Port Washington, New York: Kennikat Press., 1976, p. 123.

12. Ibid., *The Sir William Johnson Papers* Volume I., p. 721 and 733.

13. Milton W. Hamilton, *Sir William Johnson Colonial American 1715-1763*, p. 133.

14. Ibid.

15. *The Sir William Johnson Papers*, Volume I., p. XXI, introduction.

16. Ibid.

17. Ibid.

18. Ibid., p. 9.

19. Ibid.,

20. Ibid., p. XXI introduction.

21. Lawrence H. Lder ed. T*he Robert Livington Indian Records 1666-1723,* p. 77.

22. Ibid.

23. *The Sir William Johnson Papers,* Volume I., p. 6.

24. Milton W. Hamilton. *Sir William Johnson and the Indians of New York,* Albany: The University of the State of New York, State Education Department, 1967., p. 15.

25. Ibid.

26. Ibid.

27. Ibid.

28. Edward B. O'Callaghan ed. *The Documentary History of the State of*

New York, Albany: Weed Parsons and Company Publishers, 1849., Volume II., p. 691.

29. Ibid., p. 693.

30. Ibid.

31. Ibid.

32. Ibid.

33. Clifford K. Shipton and James E. Mooney ed. *National Index of American Imprints Through 1800 (Camp on Lake George, September 9, 1755, An Account of Part of the Lake George Battle by Sir William Johnson)*, American Antiquarian Society and Barre Publishers, 1969., p. 1.

34. Ibid.

35. Ibid., pp. 1-2.

36. Milton W. Hamilton. *Sir William Johnson and the Indians of New York*, pp. 15-16.

37. Clifford K. Shipton and James E. Mooney ed. N*ational Index of American Imprints Through 1800 (Camp on Lake George, September 9, 1755, An Account of Part of the Lake George Battle by Sir William Johnson)*, p. 2.

38. Ibid.

39. Ibid.

40. Ibid.

41. Ibid.

42. Ibid.

43. Ibid., p. 3.

44. Edward Bailey O'Callaghan ed., *Documents Relative to the State of New York*, Albany: Weed, Parsons and Company Printers, 1856., Volume X, p. 324.

45. Milton W. Hamilton. *Sir William Johnson Colonial American 1715-1763*, p. 165.

46. Ibid.

47. Francis Parkman. *France and England in North America*, Volume II, p. 1061.

48. Ibid., pp. 1054-1055.

49. Ibid., p. 1061.

50. Stanley McCrory Pargellis ed. *Military Affairs in North America 1748-1765*, New York City: D. Appleton-Century Company, 1936., p. 142.

51. Ibid.

52. Francis Parkman. *France and England in North America*, Volume II, p. 1059.

53. Milton W. Hamilton. *Sir William Johnson and the Indians of New York.* p. 16.

54. Augustine Buell. *Sir William Johnson,* New York: D. Appleton and Company, 1903., p. 154.

55. Louis Effingham DeForest ed. *The Journal of Seth Pomeroy Sometime General in Colonial Service,* New Haven, Connecticut: The Tuttle, Morehouse and Taylor Company, 1926., p. 143.

56. Ibid., p. 142.

57. Ibid., pp. 142-143.

58. Edward Bailey O'Callaghan ed. *Documents Relative to the State of New York*, Volume X., pp. 422-423.

59. Ibid., p. 321.

60. Ibid., p. 342.

61. Ibid.

62. Ibid.

63. Ibid.

64. Stanley McCrory Pargellis ed. *Military Affairs in North America 1748-1765*, p. 139.

65. Ibid., p. 139-141.

66. Edward Bailey O'Callaghan ed. *The Documents Relative to the State of New York*, Volume X., p. 343.

67. Arthur Pound, *Johnson of the Mohawks: A Biography of Sir William Johnson*, New York: The Macmillan Company, 1930., p. 206.

68. Ibid.

69. Milton W. Hamilton. *Sir William Johnson Colonial American 1715-1763,* p. 187.

70. *The Sir William Johnson Papers*, Volume II., p. 33.

71. Ibid.

72. *The Sir William Johnson Papers*, Volume IX., p. 386.

73. *The Sir William Johnson Papers*, Volume II, p. 425.

74. Ibid.

75. Edward Bailey O'Callaghan ed. *The Documents Relative to the State of New York*, Volume II., pp. 422-423.

76. Ibid., p. 423.

77. *The Sir William Johnson Papers*, Volume I., p. XVII, introduction.

78. Ibid.

79. Augustine Buell. *Sir William Johnson*, p. 161.

80. Ibid.

81. *The Sir William Johnson Papers*, Volume I., p. XXII, introduction.

82. Augustine Buell, *Sir William Johnson*, p. 161.

83. *The Sir William Johnson Papers*, Volume II., p. 403.

84. Milton W. Hamilton. *Sir William Johnson and the Indians of New York,* p. 21.

85. *The Sir William Johnson Papers*, Volume II., pp. 442-447.

86. Ibid., p. 443.

87. Ibid., p. 447.

88. Ibid., p. 446.

89. Ibid., p. 447.

90. Ibid.

91. Ibid.

92. James Thomas Flexner. *Lord of the Mohawks: A Biography of Sir William Johnson,* Boston: Little, Brown and Company, 1959., p. 177.

93. Ibid.

94. Charles Henry Lincoln ed. C*orrespondence of William Shirley, Governor of Massachusetts and Military Commander in America 1731-1760*, New York: The Macmillan Company., Volume II., pp. 372-374.

95. *The Sir William Johnson Papers*, Volume II., p. 710.

96. Ibid.

97. Ibid.

98. Ibid., p. 711.

99. Ibid.

100. *The Sir William Johnson Papers*, Volume I., p. XXII, introduction.

101. Ibid.

102. Ibid.

103. William Leete Stone. *The Life and Times of Sir William Johnson*, Albany: J. Munsell, 1860., Volume II., p. 12.

104. Ibid.

105. Ibid.

Also Edward Bailey O'Callaghan ed. *The Documents Relative to the State of New York*, Volume VII., pp. 117-120.

106. Ibid.

107. Augustine Buell. *Sir William Johnson*, pp. 163-166.

108. Ibid., p. 164.

109. Ibid., p. 165.

110. Francis Parkman. *France and England in North America*, Volume II., p. 1272.

111. Augustine Buell. *Sir William Johnson*, p. 165.

112. Francis Parkman. *France and England in North America*, Volume II., p. 1272.

113. Augustine Buell. *Sir William Johnson*, p. 165.

114. *The Sir William Johnson Papers*, Volume I., p. XXIV, introduction.

115. Ibid.

116. *The Sir William Johnson Papers,* Volume II., p. 667.

117. Ibid., pp. 667-668.

118. James Thomas Flexner. *Lord of the Mohawks: A Biography of Sir William Johnson*, pp. 182-187.

119. Ibid.

120. Francis Parkman. *France and England in North America*, Volume II., p. 1224.

121. Ibid.

122. Ibid.

123. Edward Bailey O'Callaghan ed., *The Documents Relative to the State of New York*, Volume X., p. 700.

124. Ibid.

125. *Proceedings and Treaties with the Shawanese, Nanticokes, Mohikanders and a few Iroquois Living at Otsiningo on one of the West Branches of the Susquehanna River Negotiated at Fort Johnson in the County of Albany in the Province of New York, April 14-23rd, 1757 by the Honourable Sir William Johnson Bart, Published by Earl of Loudoun*, New York: J. Parker and W. Weyman, 1757., p. 14.

126. Edward Bailey O'Callaghan ed. *The Documents Relative to the State of New York*, Volume X, p. 700.

127. Ibid.

128. Ibid., p. 701.

129. Francis Parkman. *France and England in North America*, pp. 1228-1229.

130. *The Sir William Johnson Papers*, Volume I., p. XXIV, introduction.

131. Milton W. Hamilton. *Sir William Johnson Colonial American*, p. 236.

132. *The Sir William Johnson Papers*, Volume I., p. XXIV, introduction.

133. Edward Bailey O'Callaghan ed. T*he Documentary History of the State of New York*, Volume X., p. 782.

134. Ibid.

135. *The Sir William Johnson Papers*, Volume I., p. XXV, introduction.

136. Edward Bailey O'Callaghan ed. *The Documents Relative to the State of New York*, Volume VII., p. 402.

137. Ibid.

138. *The Sir William Johnson Papers*, Volume III., p. 106.

139. Edward Bailey O'Callaghan ed. *The Documents Relative to the State of New York*, Volume VII., p. 402.

140. James Thomas Flexner. *Lord of the Mohawks: A Biography of Sir William Johnson*, p. 210.

141. Milton W. Hamilton. *Sir William Johnson Colonial American 1715-1763*, pp. 241-259.

142. Ibid.

143. James Thomas Flexner. *Lord of the Mohawks: A Biography of Sir William Johnson*, p. 210.

144. Edward Bailey O'Callaghan ed. *The Documentary History of the State of New York*, Volume II., pp. 791-792.

145. Ibid., p. 784.

146. Ibid.

CHAPTER 6

1. Edward B. O'Callaghan ed. *The Documentary History of the State of New York,* Albany: Weed Parson and Company Publisher, 1849., Volume II., p. 784.

2. Ibid.

3. Ibid.

4. John Knox, *A Complete History of the Late War or Annual Register of the Rise, Progress and Event in Europe, Asia and America,* Dublin: John Exshaw Publishers, 1774., p. 4.

5. Ibid.

6. Ibid., p. 5.

7. Howard H. Peckham, *The Colonial Wars 1689-1762*, Chicago and London: The University of Chicago Press, 1964., pp. 144-145.

8. Ibid., p. 145.

9. Ibid.

10. Ibid., p. 148.

11. John Knox, *A Complete History of the Late War or Annual Register of the Rise, Progress and Events in Europe, Asia and America,* Dublin: John Exshaw Publishers, 1774., p. 120.

12. Ibid.

13. Ibid.

14. Ibid., p. 121.

15. Ibid.

16. John Knox, *An Historical Journal of the Campaigns In North America for the Years 1757, 1758, 1759 and 1760,* Toronto: The Champlain Society, 1914-1916., Volume I., p. 379.

17. John Knox, *A Complete History of the Late War or Annual Register of the Rise, Progress and Events in Europe, Asia and America,* p. 186.

18. John Knox, *An Historical Journal of the Campaigns In North America for the Years 1757, 1758, 1759, and 1760,* Volume I., p. 382.

19. Ibid.

20. Ibid.

21. John Knox, *A Complete History of the Late War or Annual Register of the Rise, Progress and Events in Europe, Asia and America,* p. 186.

22. Milton W. Hamilton, *Sir William Johnson Colonial American 1715-1763,* Port Washington, New York: Kennikat Press., 1976, pp. 241-259.

23. Francis Parkman, *France and England in North America,* New York: Literary Classics of the United States, Inc., 1983., Volume II, pp. 1368.

24. Ibid.

25. Ibid.

26. Ibid.

27. Arthur Pound, *Johnson of the Mohawks: A Biography of Sir William Johnson,* New York: The Macmillan Company, 1930., p. 284.

28. Ibid.

29. Ibid.

30. John Knox, *An Historical Journal of the Campaigns In North America for the Years 1757, 1758, 1759, and 1760,* Volume II., pp. 71 and 80.

31. *The Sir William Johnson Papers*, Albany: The University of the State of New York., 1921-1965, Volume III, pp. 197, 199 and 201. Also Milton W. Hamilton, *Sir William Johnson Colonial American 1715-1763*, p. 271.

32. Ibid.

33. John Knox, *An Historical Journal of the Campaigns In North America for the Years 1757, 1758, 1759 and 1760,* Volume II., p. 384.

34. Ibid., p. 400.

35. Ibid.

36. Ibid.

37. Ibid.

38. Ibid.

39. *The Sir William Johnson Papers,* Volume III, pp. 269-275.

40. Milton W. Hamilton, *Sir William Johnson Colonial American 1715-1763*, p. 273.

41. Howard H. Peckham, *The Colonial Wars 1689-1762*, pp. 198-199.

42. Herbert L. Osgood, *The American Colonies In the Eighteenth Century,* Gloucester, Massachusetts: Peter Smith., Volume IV, p. 457.

43. John Knox, *A Complete History of the Late War or Annual Register of the Rise, Progress and Events in Europe, Asia and America,* p. 408.

44. Ibid.

45. John Knox, *An Historical Journal of Campaigns In North America for the Years 1757, 1758, 1759 and 1760,,* Volume II, p. 384.

46. *The Sir William Johnson Papers,* Volume III, pp. 269-275.

47. Howard H. Peckham, *The Colonial Wars 1689-1762*, pp. 160-161.

48. Milton W. Hamilton, *Sir William Johnson Colonial American 1715-1763*, p. 63.

49. Ibid.

50. *The Sir William Johnson Papers,* Volume I, pp. 90-92.

Also Milton W. Hamilton, *Sir William Johnson Colonial American 1715-1763*, p. 63.

51. Edward B. O'Callaghan ed., *Documents Relative to the State of New York,* Albany: Weed, Parsons and Company Printers, 1856., Volume VI, p. 965 and p. 984.

52. Ibid.

53. James Thomas Flexner, *Lord of the Mohawks: A Biography of Sir William Johnson,* Boston: Little Brown and Company, 1959., p. 76.

54. Milton W. Hamilton, *Sir William Johnson Colonial American 1715-1763,* p. 190.

55. Arthur Pound, *Johnson of the Mohawks: A Biography of Sir William Johnson,* pp. 120-122.

56. Ibid., p. 121.

57. Ibid., pp. 120-122.

58. Ibid., p. 479.

59. Ibid.

60. Milton W. Hamilton, *Sir William Johnson Colonial American 1715-1763,* p. 126.

61. Ibid.

62. *The Sir William Johnson Papers,* Volume I, pp. 475-476.

63. Ibid., Introduction, p. xx.

64. Ibid.

65. Milton W. Hamilton, *Sir William Johnson Colonial American 1715-1763,* p. 128.

66. Edward B. O'Callaghan ed., *Documents Relative to the State of New York,* Volume VI, p. 973.

67. Ibid., p. 961.

68. Milton W. Hamilton, *Sir William Johnson Colonial American 1715-1763,* p. 126.

69. Ibid.

70. Ibid.

71. Ibid., pp. 125-126.

72. Arthur Pound, *Johnson of the Mohawks: A Biography of Sir William Johnson,* p. 481.

73. Milton W. Hamilton, *Sir William Johnson Colonial American 1715-1763,* p. 337.

74. *The Sir William Johnson Papers,* Volume I, p. 153.

75. Ibid.

76. Ibid.

77. Ibid.

78. Ibid.

79. Ibid.

80. Ibid., pp. 155-156.

81. George Laurence Gomme ed., "The Gentleman's Magazine - Topographical History 1732-1868", London: E. Stock, 1756, Volume 26., p. 404.

82. Arthur Pound, *Johnson of the Mohawks: A Biography of Sir William Johnson,* pp. 7-9.

83. Ibid., p. 9.

84. Ibid., p. 10.

85. Ibid.

86. Sidney Hook, *The Hero In History,* Boston: The Beacon Press, 1943., p. 153.

87. Ibid.

88. Ibid., p. 157.

89. John Knox, *A Complete History of the Late War or Annual Register of the Rise, Progress and Events in Europe, Asia and America,* p. 408.

90. Ibid., p. 186.

91. Ibid.

92. Ibid., p. 408.

93. *The Sir William Johnson Papers,* Volume III, p. 28.

BIBLIOGRAPHY

Primary Sources

An Account of the Conference held and the treaties made between General Sir William Johnson and the chief sachems and warriors of North Americans at Fort Johnson's in the years 1755-1756, (with a letter from Reverend Mr. Hawley to Sir William Johnson), London: A. Millar, 1756, 77 pp.

> This is a valuable primary source that provided insights on the Indians of North America and especially those living in the Northeast. It also gave accounts of Sir William Johnson's influence over his Native American brothers. For this reason, this volume was of great interest.

An Account of Conferences held and Treaties made Between Major-General Sir William Johnson, Bart and the Chief Sachems and Warriors of the Mohawks, Oneidas, Onondagas, Cayugas, Senekas, Tuskaroras, Aughquageys, Skaniadaradighronos, Chugnuts, Mahickanders, Shawanefe, Kanus Kagos, Toderigbronos and Ogbquagoes, London: Printed for A. Millar in the Strand, 1756., 77 pp.

> This account of the conferences and treaties made between Sir William Johnson and various Indian nations was a very valuable primary source. It was used extensively to prove that Johnson influenced the Iroquois and other Indians to side with the British and fight the French during the French and Indian War.

Benson, Adolph B. Peter Kalm's *Travels In North America; The America of 1750 (Revised and Translated from the original Swedish)*, New York: Wilson-Erickson, Inc., 1937., 380 pp.

This very valuable primary source provided insight into New York only a few years after Sir William Johnson moved from Ireland. It was important for the early portion of my project. Peter Kalm's description of Albany was of great interest.

Claus, Daniel. *Narrative of his Relations with Sir William Johnson and Experiences of the Lake George Fight*, New York: Printed by order of the Society of Colonial Wars, 1904., 40 pp.

This short volume was written by a man who lived at the time of Sir William Johnson and shared experiences with him. It presented insights into how another individual viewed the famous New Yorker. It also gave valuable information on the Battle of Lake George. It is an important primary source.

Colden, Cadwalder. *The History of the Five Nations of Canada*, London: Lockyer Davis., 1755, 2 volumes.

Colden's work discusses the history of the Iroquois during the Sir William Johnson era. It includes very valuable information on the Iroquois Confederation and on the influence these Indians had on the French and Indian War. I consulted the volume often, especially for Chapter Two of this project, on the Six Nations.

DeForest, Louis Effingham ed., *The Journal and Papers of Seth Pomeroy, Sometime General in Colonial Service*, New Haven, Connecticut: The Tuttle, Morehouse and Taylor Company, 1926., 180 pp.

Seth Pomeroy fought in the Battle of Lake George in which Sir William Johnson, although wounded, defeated the British leader Baron Dieskau. Dieskau was taken captive and later Johnson was made a baronet.

Pomeroy's journal gave insights into the Lake George battle and was an invaluable source. It was used extensively when the battle was discussed.

Gomme, George Laurence ed., *"The Gentleman's Magazine - Topographical History 1731-1868"*, London: E. Stock, 1756, Volume 26., 618 pp.

This British magazine has short sections that mention Sir William Johnson and the Iroquois. It contained insights into how British society viewed the famed New Yorker. It was a valuable primary source.

Hamilton, Milton Wheaton ed. *Letters to the Governors, Lake George September 9-10, 1755*, American Antiquarian Society, Worchester, Massachusetts, 1964.

These letters were valuable to me because they were sent during two days of the French and Indian War. I consulted them to get background on the war. They provided information in a short period in the most important colonial war in our history.

Katz, Stanley Nider ed. *Newcastle's New York: Anglo-American Politics 1732-1753* Cambridge, Massachusetts: Belkap Press of Harvard University Press, 1968., 244 pp.

Newcastle's volume discusses the political arena in the British American colonies during Sir William Johnson's time. It presented valuable information on the political situation in New York during the period of this book. I referred to it often.

Knox, John. *A Complete History of the Late War or Annual Register of the Rise, Progress and Events in Europe, Asia, Africa and America*, Dublin: John Exshaw Publishers, 1774., 625 pp.

This extremely important primary source contains a record of the events of the French and Indian War. It includes all the important events that led up to the war and the battles that occurred. Sir William Johnson and his part in the war are mentioned numerous times. The information contained was used extensively for the later portions of this volume. This was especially the case in Chapter Six of this project, when Sir William Johnson's total effect on the French and Indian War is discussed.

Knox, Captain John (d. 1778), *An Historical Journal of the Campaigns In North America for the Years 1757, 1758, and 1759 and 1760*, London: Printed by the Author, 1769., 2 volumes.

This is a valuable primary source on the French and Indian War era. It covers many events that were important to my volume topic. I used it extensively for the last two chapters of my project. At times, I relied on this source for real insight into the role Sir William Johnson played in the war.

Lder, Lawrence H. ed. T*he Robert Livington Indian Records* 1666-1723, Gettysburg, Pennsylvania: The Pennsylvania Historical Association, 1956., 537 pp.

Lder's edition contains some valuable Indian records that were used for Chapter Two of my volume on the Iroquois Indians. The only real shortcoming of the source is that it only traces Indian history to 1723. My project chronicles the Iroquois until approximately 1760. Other sources were needed to supplement the Livington records to chronicle the Iroquois up to the French and Indian War period.

Lincoln, Charles Henry, ed., *A Calendar of Manuscripts*, American Antiquarian Society: Worchester, Massachusetts, 1907.

> This collection of documents was one of the most important and valuable sources that I consulted. It includes a number of primary documents that I used extensively. Much of the information contained is on the French and Indian War era. Therefore, the source was important for this volume.

Lincoln, Charles Henry ed., *Correspondence of William Shirley, Governor of Massachusetts and Military Commander in America 1731-1760*, New York: The Macmillan Company., Vol, I and II., 1912.

> This two volume source was important to my topic because it mentioned Sir William Johnson a number of times. Governor Shirley corresponded with Johnson generally on the topic of the Indians. Shirley and Johnson did not see eye to eye, which is somewhat obvious from the documents. This made the source very interesting.

Livingston, William ed. *Review of the Military Operations in North America; From the Commencement of the French Hostilities on the Frontiers of Virginia in 1753, to the Surrender of Oswego on the 14th of August, 1756*, Dublin: Printed for P. Wilson, and J. Exshaw., 1757., 276 pp.

> This primary source chronicles the early operations of the French and Indian War. It covers the years 1753 to 1756 and mentions many topics that were important for my project. It was very valuable and was used extensively.

Madden, Samuel. *Reflections ad Resolutions Proper for the Gentlemen of Ireland, As to their Conduct for the Service of their Company*, Dublin: R. Reilly for George Ewing., 1738., 224 pp.

> Madden's volume, written during Sir William Johnson's lifetime, discusses proper conduct in Ireland during the early eighteenth century. It contained information regard-

ing what was considered proper for young men in Ireland
during Sir William Johnson's early life. I found the volume
valuable for the first chapter of this book.

McIlwain, Charles Howard ed. *An Abridgement of the Indian Affairs
Contained in Four Volumes, Transacted in the Colony of New York,
From the Year 1678 to the Year 1751 by Peter Wraxall*, New York
and London: Benjamin Blom, 1968., 251 pp.

McIlwain's edition was a valuable source on Indian affairs
and Indian history in New York up to 1751. I referred to it
extensively and quoted it often. I found the volume
extremely informative and interesting, although somewhat biased, because it was compiled by Peter Wraxall,
Sir William Johnson's secretary and friend.

O'Callaghan, Edward Bailey ed. *The Documents Relative to the State
of New York*, (Procured in Holland, England and France by John
Romeyn Brodhead Esquire), Albany: Weed, Parsons and Company
Printers, 1856., Volumes II, VI, VII, X, and XI.

This source includes many letters concerning Sir William
Johnson's influence on the Indians of the New York area
and in general. My volume concerns Johnson's influence.
Therefore, the source was valuable for my project.

O'Callaghan, Edward Bailey. ed. *The Documentary History of the State
of New York*, Albany: Weed, Parsons and Company Publishers,
1849., Volumes I, II, III, and X.

This was an extremely valuable primary source. Only the
Sir William Johnson Papers were better. I used the
Documentary History extensively and quoted from it
numerous times. Many events that were important to my
project are discussed in this source. Also, Sir William
Johnson is mentioned on many pages. However, at times,
The Documentary History contains the same information
found in the Johnson Papers.

*Proceedings and Treaty with the Shawanefe, Nanticokes and
Mohikander Indians Living at Otsiningo on one of the West
Branches of the Susquehanna River Negotiated at Fort Johnson in
the County of Albany in the Province of New York, April 14-23 1757,
by the Honourable Sir William Johnson Bart*. Published by the
Honourable John Earl of Loudoun, New York: J. Parker and W.
Weyman, 1757., 14 pp.

This valuable source presented insights into Sir William

Johnson's relationship with the Indians. It mainly covered his relations with Indians who were not part of the powerful Iroquois Confederation. Sir William's influence on Indians in general is important to my topic. This is why I included this source in my bibliography.

Recum, Franz von. *The Families of Warren and Johnson of Warrenstown*, County Meath, Ireland, New York: The New York Historical Society, 1950., 9 pp.

This short selection gives important information on the genealogy of the Warren and Johnson families of Meath County, Ireland. It was valuable for the early part of my project. It revealed that Sir William Johnson was of the gentry class and that this helped him in his future endeavors.

Rogers, Robert, *Ponteach: or the Savages of America A Tragedy*, London: Printed by the author and sold by J. Millan, 1766., 110 pp.

This play by Robert Rogers reveals the prejudice that existed toward the Indians in colonial America. I referred to it extensively to get a thorough understanding on the topic. I also quoted Rogers a number of times in Chapter Two of this volume.

Shipton, Clifford K., and Mooney, James E. ed. *National Index of American Imprints Through 1800 (Camp on Lake George, September 9, 1755, An Account of part of the Lake George Battle by Sir William Johnson)*, American Antiquarian Society and Barre Publishers, 1969., on Microfiche., 3 pp.

This short account of the battle of Lake George, during the French and Indian War, provided invaluable information into Sir William Johnson's military exploits. It also mentioned the use of Indians by the famed New Yorker. It was very valuable for this volume.

Sir William Johnson Papers, (Prepared for publication by the Division of Archives and History), Albany: The University of the State of New York, 1921-1965., 14 volumes.

This series of volumes was my best and most interesting source. It contains all the correspondence sent and received by Sir William Johnson. It was of great value for my project. Anyone doing research on Sir William will find extensive information in this source. I relied on the *Sir William Johnson Papers* to a very great extent.

Stanley McCrory Pargellis ed. *Military Affairs in North America 1748-1765*, New York City: D. Appleton-Century Company, 1936., 514 pp.

Pargellis' edition is a valuable primary source which records the military affairs of the French and Indian War. It was used extensively for the later chapters of this project. It contains important information that provided tremendous insights into the day to day activity of the last colonial war between Britain and France.

Stokes, George T. ed. *Pococke's Tour in Ireland in 1752*, Dublin: Hodges, Figgis and Company., 1981., 187 pp.

Pococke's 1752 tour reveals information on Ireland only two decades after Sir William Johnson lived there. It gave me insights into the early home of my main character. It was a valuable source that was used for the early section of this volume.

The Letters and Papers of Caldwalder Colden, New York: Printed for the New York Historical Society, Volume 9, 1937., 434 pp.

Caldwalder Colden was a noted colonial figure during Sir William Johnson's time. He also wrote *A History of The Five Nations* which was consulted for Chapter Two of this dissertation. The Colden Papers were valuable for this project because they mentioned Sir William and others who lived during the time. The source was important, mainly to understand the relationship between Sir William Johnson and Governor George Clinton during the era of King George's War.

Young, Arthur. *A Tour in Ireland with General Observations on the Present State of that Kingdom Made in the Years 1776, 1777, 1778 and 1779,* Dublin: George Bohham, 1780., 416 pp.

Young's volume discusses Ireland during the 1770's. Sir William Johnson lived there many years before this time and left for New York in 1737. However, Young's observations are somewhat valuable, for they contained a fair estimate of the Ireland in which Sir William Johnson lived.

Secondary Sources

Bond, Richard P. *Queen Anne's American Kings*, Oxford: The Clarendon Press, 1952., 91 pp.

Bond's book discusses the four Iroquois Sachems who visited England in 1710. They were not kings in the traditional sense, but were received with honor by the British Crown. The volume was not of great value for my topic, but did provide some basic background on a specific aspect of Iroquois history.

Bryce, Peter H. *"Sir William Johnson Bart.: The Great Diplomat of the British-French Frontier"*, *New York State Historical Association Quarterly Journal*, VIII, October, 1927., pp. 352-373.

This article discusses the diplomatic services that Sir William Johnson performed in order to keep North America under British control. The article largely discusses Johnson's influence and diplomacy with the Indians in keeping the numerous tribes neutral or on the side of the British during the French and Indian War. For this reason, I found this article interesting and valuable to my volume.

Buell, Augustine. *Sir William Johnson*, New York: D. Appleton and Company, 1903., 281 pp.

This is a good secondary source with much valuable information on my subject. I read the whole book and did get insight into the period of my volume. For this reason, I would recommend Buell's biography.

Cusick, David. *Sketches of Ancient History of the Six Nations*, Tuscarora Village: Lewiston, Niagara Company, 1828., 36 pp.

This fanciful history of the ancient Iroquois contains some valuable legends about the Six Nations. I did not find Cusick's volume of historical sketches valuable for my volume. However, I did refer to it to gain information on the folklore of the early Iroquois. It was of minor value for my project.

Doughty, Howard. *Francis Parkman*, New York: The Macmillan Company, 1962., 403 pp.

This biography of historian Francis Parkman gave insight into his view of history. It gave me background into Parkman's view of Native Americans in the grand scheme of things and in the march of civilization.

Drake, Samuel. *A Particular History of the Five Years French and Indian War*, (With a Memoir of Major-General Shirley), Freeport, New York: Books for Libraries Press, 1970, 300 pp.

Although this is a secondary source, it does contain some primary material. For this reason, the volume was of fair value for this book.

Ellis, David M.; Frost, James A.; Carman, Harry F. *A Short History of New York State*, Ithaca, New York: Cornell University Press, 1962., 653 pp.

This basic volume covers the history of New York State from earliest times until the 1960's. I consulted it to gain background for my project. It also provided valuable assistance in keeping my story chronologically correct.

Flexner, James Thomas. *Lord of the Mohawks: A Biography of Sir William Johnson,* Boston: Little Brown and Company, 1959., 356 pp.

Flexner's biography is probably the most interesting volume I consulted on my main character. The only trouble is that the volume is not well documented and reads more like a novel than a work of history. Flexner made Johnson a folk hero more than a flesh and blood human being. I felt as background material, the book was only of fair value. Dr. Hamilton's volume on Johnson is probably much closer to the real person who roamed the forests of New York and influenced much of colonial history.

Fox, Edith Mead. *William Johnson's early career as a Frontier Landlord and Trader*, Ithaca, New York, (M.A. Thesis at Cornell University), 1945., 137 pp.

This rather short volume discusses Sir William Johnson's early career. It provided valuable background on this phase of his life. My research covered, in part, Sir William's early life and career. Because of this, Fox's Masters thesis was of value for my project.

Hamilton, Edward P. *The French and Indian Wars*, Garden City, New York: Doubleday and Company, 1962., 306 pp.

This volume contains background on the colonial wars between France and Britain. It covers all four wars, but contains valuable information on the French and Indian War. For this reason, I found the volume of interest. It was of fair value for my project.

Hamilton, Milton W. *Sir William Johnson Colonial American 1715-1763*, Port Washington, New York: Kennikat Press, 1976., 332 pp.

This was the best secondary source I consulted. It contains all the important aspects of Sir William Johnson's life and added a few points that other sources left out. I consulted it often for chronological perspective in writing this dissertation. I studied Dr. Hamilton's bibliography and footnotes to gain insight in what sources to consult on Johnson's early life. I also quoted the volume a number of times.

Hamilton's volume is thoroughly documented and is obviously a work researched and written by a first-rate historian. The work is head and shoulders above any other biography I consulted.

Hamilton, Milton Wheaton. *Sir William Johnson and the Indians of New York,* Albany: The University of the State of New York, State Education Department, 1967., 47 pp.

This short selection gives insight into Sir William Johnson's relationship with the Indians. My project concerns Sir William's influence on Native Americans during his time. I found Hamilton's volume added to my understanding and knowledge of this influence. For that reason, it was valuable to my project.

Hamilton, Milton W. *"Sir William Johnson's Wives"*, New York History, XXXVIII, January, 1957., pp. 18-28.

Hamilton discusses the main females that Sir William cohabited with during his lifetime. All of these ladies may not have been official wives, but are discussed as just that in this article. The article is very well done and very informative. I used it extensively for the early portion of this volume. It was one of my most valuable secondary sources.

Hook, Sidney. *The Hero In History*, Boston: The Beacon Press, 1943., 267 pp.

Hook discusses two kinds of heroes. First was the eventful man who supposedly pulled history along, but did not necessarily change its outcome. Second was the event-making man who changed the course of history. This person was the real hero in history. Sir William Johnson was very possibly an event-making man.

Hunt, George T. *The Wars of the Iroquois*, Madison: The University of Wisconsin Press, 1940., 181 pp.

Hunt's volume was one of my best sources on the

Iroquois. It discusses extensively how the Iroquois became the most powerful organization of Indians in United States history. I referred to the volume often for Chapter Two of this volume.

Jacob, Wilbur R. *Wilderness Politics and Indian Gifts: The Northern Colonial Frontier 1748-1763*, Lincoln, Nebraska: The University of Nebraska Press, 1966., 185 pp.

This basic text on the Northern frontier from 1748-1763 has many pages devoted to Sir William Johnson. It was of fair value for my project because of this as background information.

Lloyd, Peter. *The Emergence of a Racial Prejudice Toward the Indians in Seventeenth Century New England*, A Doctoral Dissertation At Ohio State University, 1975, 224 pp.

Lloyd's dissertation gave me valuable background on the racial prejudice the Europeans expressed toward the Indians of New England and thus throughout the British colonies. The insight Lloyd's work contains expanded my understanding of the true nature of the problem. I found the work informative and interesting.

Lydekker, John Wolfe. *The Faithful Mohawks*, New York: The Macmillan Company, 1938., 189 pp.

Lydekker's volume contains some important information on the Mohawks, one of the six nations of Iroquois. I used it to some extent as background material for my volume.

Morgan, Lewis H. *Ho-Dè-No-Sau-Nee or Iroquois*, New York: Dodd, Mead and Company, 2 Volumes, 1901., 306 pp.

Morgan's volume is an excellent source on the history of the Six Nations of Iroquois. It contained valuable background on the Iroquois Confederation. I used this source extensively for Chapter two of my volume.

Morris, Richard B., ed. *Encyclopedia of American History*, New York: Harper and Row Publishers, 1965., 808 pp.

This basic reference book on American History was used for chronology for this volume. I referred to it a number of times.

Osgood, Herbert L. *The American Colonies In the Eighteenth Century*, Gloucester, Massachusetts: Peter Smith, 1958., 4 Volumes.

This basic survey history contains a number of pages on Sir William Johnson and the battles he took part in during the French and Indian War. The volume was of some value as background material for my project. It also helped me keep the chronology correct when writing on the French and Indian War period.

Parker, Arthur C. *The Constitution of the Five Nations,* Albany: The University of the State of New York, 1916., 151 pp.

Parker's volume gave me background on the basic laws of the Iroquois Confederation. It provided insight into the culture of the Iroquois. I found it somewhat valuable in my understanding of the Confederation of the Six Nations.

Parkman, Francis. *France and England In North America*, Boston: Little Brown and Company, Volume II, 1892., 333 pp.

Francis Parkman is considered one of the acknowledged historians on the colonial wars between France and Britain. I found the source invaluable and consulted it often. It has many pages devoted to Sir William Johnson and the Iroquois. The only shortcoming of the volume is that Parkman is very biased toward Johnson and many times looks negatively on his exploits.

Parkman, Francis. *Montcalm and Wolfe; France and England in North America Part VII,* Boston: Little Publishers, 1884., 2 volumes.

This excellent source gives the military setting for Johnson's activities during the French and Indian War. It is based on the records of the time. It was very valuable in giving me the proper chronology of Sir William Johnson's role against the French. The only shortcoming is that Parkman was very biased toward Johnson and reveals that numerous times in his writing.

Peckham, Howard H. *The Colonial Wars 1689-1762*, Chicago and London: The University of Chicago Press, 1964., 221 pp.

This is an excellent secondary source. I consulted it to get background and to help me with the chronology of the French and Indian War.

Pound, Arthur. Johnson of the Mohawks: *A Biography of Sir William Johnson*, New York: The Macmillan Company, 1930., 556 pp.

This was a good basic biography of the famed New

Yorker. I consulted it often, especially for information on Johnson's early life. I also used it extensively for the later portions of my volume.

Reid, William Maxwell. *The Story of Old Fort Johnson*, New York and London: G.P. Putnam and Sons, 1906., 240 pp.

This secondary source gave background on Old Fort Johnson and Sir William Johnson. I consulted it a few times. It had limited value for my project.

The volume mixes fact and legend about Johnson. I found the book interesting, but not always dealing with the facts. For instance, Johnson's frustrated love affair in Ireland is written about in the volume. This is not mentioned in any of the primary material I consulted. Also, in his preface, the author states his work is the story of Old Fort Johnson, but, in actuality, the book is a biography of Sir William Johnson, for Johnson is mentioned on almost every page.

Ritchie, William. *Indian History of New York State Volume 2*, The Iroquoian Tribes, Albany, 1953

Ritchie's volume is a basic history of the Indians of New York State. I used it to gain background on the subject. It was valuable for my volume in a minor way.

Shutz, John A. *William Shirley, King's Governor of Massachusetts*, Chapel Hill: The University of North Carolina Press, 1961., 271 pp.

This biography of William Shirley contains information on Sir William Johnson. Shirley and Johnson corresponded numerous times during the French and Indian War period. For this reason, this secondary source was of some value for my project. Also, this source gave me insight into the understanding and use of *The William Shirley Papers.*

Severence, Frank Hayward. *An Old Frontier of France; the Niagara Region and Adjacent Lakes under French Control*, New York: Dodd Publishers, 1917., 2 volumes.

These volumes delve into French control and influence during the French and Indian War. It has a number of pages that reveal the French attempt to undermine Sir William Johnson's influence with the Six Nations of the Iroquois Confederation. It must be remembered that Sir William worked hardest in keeping the Iroquois fighting

with the British. The French tried to counteract this influence and get the Indians to fight with them. As background material on the French, this volume was very
valuable.

Seymour, Flora Warren, *Lord of the Valley: Sir William Johnson and
His Mohawk Brothers*, London and New York: Longmans, Green
and Company, 1930., 278 pp.

This basic biography of the famed New Yorker was valuable as background material. The volume stresses Sir
William Johnson's relationship with his Mohawk brothers
as well as to Indians in general. My project deals with this
topic. Therefore, the volume was of fair importance for
my book. The only drawback is that the volume does not
always separate fact from legend concerning the famed
New Yorker.

Simms, Jeptha Root. *Trappers of Old New York or Nicholas Stoner and
Nathaniel Foster; together with accounts of Sir William Johnson*,
Albany; J. Munsell, 1860., 287 pp.

This dated secondary source contains a number of pages
on the exploits of Sir William Johnson. It was not nearly
the best secondary source I consulted. The modern
biographies by such men as Pound and Hamilton were far
better sources. However, I did consult this volume
numerous times and thus included it in this bibliography.

Smith, William. *The History of the Province of New York From the First
Discovery*, London: Printed by J. Alwon, 1776., 324 pp.

This descriptive history of New York Province gave some
background on the Johnson era. It does not contain information on Johnson, but does mention the Iroquois,
Oswego trade and other aspects important for my project.

Stone, William. *The Life of Joseph Brant*, New York: Alexander V.
Blake, 1838., 2 Volumes.

Joseph Brant was a great Mohawk Chief and brother of
Molly Brant, Sir William Johnson's live-in mistress. Sir
William became very fond of young Joseph and shared a
close relationship with the younger man throughout
much of his life. The volumes gave valuable background
on this relationship and on other aspects of Johnson's
life.

Stone, William Leete. *The Life and Times of Sir William Johnson*, Albany: J. Munsell, 1860., 2 Volumes.

Stone's two-volume work is an excellent biography of Sir William Johnson. I consulted it often and found it extremely valuable. The only shortcoming to Stone's work is that it is somewhat dated. It was published in 1860. Since that time, modern methods have revealed new material on Johnson and the Iroquois. Also, at times, Stone made obvious mistakes because he mis-read the early documents.

Trelease, Allen W. *Indian Affairs in Colonial New York: The Seventeenth Century*, Ithaca, New York: Cornell University Press, 1960., 363 pp.

Trelease's volume is a very basic work on Indian affairs generally in colonial New York. I used this source as background material on Chapter Two of this volume. It was of minor value.

Wallace, Anthony F.D. "Origins of Iroquois Neutrality: The Grand Settlement of 1701", Pennsylvania History, XXIV, July, 1957., pp. 223-235.

This article by Anthony Wallace gives a survey of the reasons why the Iroquois became neutral after King William's War. After this time, for many years, they generally did not side with Britain or France in the domination of North America. Wallace's article is a particularly good one. I referred to it numerous times.

Wallace, Paul A.W. *Conrad Weiser 1696-1760, Friend of Colonist and Mohawk*, London: Oxford University Press, 1945., 648 pp.

Conrad Weiser was an important colonial character and contemporary of Sir William Johnson. Weiser was mentioned in my volume. I consulted Wallace's volume to get a better understanding of this important character. Therefore, this source was of fair value for my project.

Wallace, Paul A. W. *The White Roots of Peace*, Philadelphia: The University of Pennsylvania Press, 1946., 57 pp.

Wallace's volume was one of my best sources on the Iroquois. I referred to it extensively when researching Chapter Two of this volume. Wallace gives valuable background on the history of the Six Nations. I referred to it often.